CW00552410

中国国家汉办赠送
Donated by Hanban,China

Wise Men Talking Series

MO ZI Says

墨子说

蔡希勤 编注

□ 责任编辑 韩颖

□ 翻译 郭辉

□ 绘图 李士伋

老人家说系列丛书

华语教学出版社
SINOLINGUA

First Edition   2011

ISBN 978 – 7 – 5138 – 0145 – 4
Copyright 2011 by Sinolingua
Published by Sinolingua
24 Baiwanzhuang Road, Beijing 100037, China
Tel: (86) 10 – 68320585 68997826
Fax: (86) 10 – 68997826 68326333
http: //www. sinolingua. com. cn
E-mail: hyjx@ sinolingua. com. cn
Printed by Beijing Songyuan Printing Co. , Ltd.

Printed in the People's Republic of China

老人家说

Wise Men Talking

俗曰:"不听老人言,吃亏在眼前。"

老人家走的路多,吃的饭多,看的书多,经的事多,享的福多,受的罪多,可谓见多识广,有丰富的生活经验,老人家说的话多是经验之谈,后生小子不可不听也。

在中国历史上,春秋战国时期是中国古代思想高度发展的时期,那个时候诸子并起,百家争鸣,出现了很多"子"字辈的老人家,他们有道家、儒家、墨家、名家、法家、兵家、阴阳家,多不胜数,车载斗量,一时星河灿烂。

后来各家各派的代表曾先后聚集于齐国稷下学宫。齐宣王是个开明的诸侯王,因纳无盐丑女钟离春为后而名声大噪。他对各国来讲学的专家学者不问来路一律管吃管住,给予政府津贴。对愿留下来做官的,授之以客卿,造巨室,付万钟;对不愿做官的,也给予"不治事而议论"之特殊待遇。果然这些人各为其主,各为其派,百家争鸣,百花齐放,设坛辩论,著书立说:有的说仁,有的说义,有的说无为,有的说逍遥,有的说非攻,有的说谋攻,有的说性善,有的说性恶,有的说亲非亲,有的说马非马,知彼知己,仁者无敌……留下了很多光辉灿烂的学术经典。

可惜好景不长,秦始皇时丞相李斯递话说"焚书坑儒",结果除秦记、医药、卜筮、种树书外,民间所藏诗、书及百家典籍均被一把火烧个精光。到西汉武帝时,董仲舒又上书提出"罢黜百家,独尊儒术",从此,儒学成了正统,"黄老、刑名百家之言"成为邪说。

"有德者必有言",儒学以外的各家各派虽屡被扫荡,却不断变换着生存方式以求不灭,并为我们保存下了十分丰富的经典著作。在这些经典里,先哲们留下了很多充满智慧和哲理的、至今仍然熠熠发光的至理名言,我们将这些各家各派的老人家的"金玉良言"编辑成这套《老人家说》丛书,加以注释并译成英文,采取汉英对照方式出版,以飨海内外有心有意于中国传统文化的广大读者。

As the saying goes, "If an old dog barks, he gives counsel. "

Old men, who walk more roads, eat more rice, read more books, have more experiences, enjoy more happiness, and endure more sufferings, are experienced and knowledgeable, with rich life experience. Thus, what they say is mostly wise counsel, and young people should listen to them.

The Spring and Autumn (770 - 476 BC) and Warring States (475 - 221 BC) periods of Chinese history were a golden age for ancient Chinese thought. In those periods, various schools of thought, together with many sages whose names bore the honorific suffix "Zi," emerged and contended, including the Taoist school, Confucian school, Mohist school, school of Logicians, Legalist school, Military school and Yin-Yang school. Numerous and well known, these schools of thought were as brilliant as the Milky Way.

Later representatives of these schools of thought flocked to the Jixia Academy of the State of Qi. Duke Xuan of Qi was an enlightened ruler, famous for making an ugly but brilliant woman his empress. The duke provided board and lodging, as well as government subsidies for experts and scholars coming to give lectures, and never inquired about their backgrounds. For those willing to hold official positions, the duke appointed them guest officials, built mansions for them and paid them high salaries. Those unwilling to take up official posts were kept on as advisors. This was an era when "one hundred schools of thought contended and a hundred flowers blossomed." The scholars debated in forums, and wrote books to expound their doctrines: Some preached benevolence; some, righteousness; some, inaction; some, absolute freedom; some, aversion to offensive war; some, attack by stratagem; some, the goodness of man's nature; some, the evil nature of man. Some said that relatives were not relatives; some said that horses were not horses; some urged the importance of knowing oneself and one's enemy; some said that benevolence knew no enemy ... And they left behind many splendid classic works of scholarship.

Unfortunately, this situation did not last long. When Qin Shihuang (reigned 221 – 210 BC) united all the states of China, and ruled as the First Emperor, his prime minister, Li Si, ordered that all books except those on medicine, fortune telling and tree planting be burned. So, all poetry collections and the classics of the various schools of thought were destroyed. Emperor Wu (reigned 140 – 88 BC) of the Western Han Dynasty made Confucianism the orthodox doctrine of the state, while other schools of thought, including the Taoist and Legalist schools, were deemed heretical.

These other schools, however, managed to survive, and an abundance of their classical works have been handed down to us. These classical works contain many wise sayings and profound insights into philosophical theory which are still worthy of study today. We have compiled these nuggets of wisdom uttered by old men of the various ancient schools of thought into this series Wise Men Talking, and added explanatory notes and English translation for the benefit of both Chinese and overseas readers fond of traditional Chinese culture.

目录

CONTENTS

What is not righteous and what is not reasonable should not be practised.

不义不富，不义不贵〔12〕

The unrighteous shall not be granted wealth, the unrighteous shall not be honoured.

C

仓无备粟，不可以待凶饥〔14〕

Famine cannot be prepared against unless there are grains stored in the granaries.

藏于心者，无以竭爱〔16〕

For the superior man, inside his heart there is endless love.

臣下重其爵位而不言，近臣则喑，远臣则唫〔18〕

If ministers value their positions and are afraid to speak their mind, whether near at hand or far away from the ruler, they will keep their silence.

D

大国之攻小国，譬犹童子之为马也〔20〕

Large states attacking smaller ones are like boys riding on bamboo sticks as horses.

大国之攻小国也，是交相贼也〔22〕

2

The attack by a large state on a small state injures both.

得意，贤士不可不举；不得意，贤士不可不举〔24〕
The virtuous must be exalted in peace and war.

F

非无安居也，我无安心也〔26〕
It is not that one has no comfortable abode but that one has no peaceful mind.

夫义，天下之大器也〔28〕
Righteousness is the greatest thing on earth.

富贵者奢侈，孤寡者冻馁〔30〕
The rich and high in rank are wasteful and extravagant, while the solitary and miserable are hungry and cold.

G

甘瓜苦蒂，天下物无全美〔32〕
The sweet melon has a bitter base near its stem. Nothing is perfect in every way in the world.

甘井近竭，招木近伐〔34〕
The sweet wells become sooner exhausted and the tall trees are oftener felled.

古者圣王之政，列德而尚贤〔36〕

In administering the government, the ancient sage kings ranked the morally excellent high and exalted the virtuous.

古者圣王甚尊尚贤而任使能〔38〕

The ancient sage kings exalted the virtuous and promoted the capable.

古之学者，得一善言附于其身〔40〕

The learned men in the ancient times earnestly practised the good and wise advice they received.

官无常贵，而民无终贱〔42〕

Officials cannot be in constant honour, and ordinary people in eternal humbleness.

国有贤良之士众，则国家之治厚〔44〕

When the virtuous are numerous in the state, the foundation of the state is solid.

国之治也，治之，故治也〔46〕

A country is politically stable, because it is well governed.

H

何以知尚贤之为政本也〔48〕

How do we know exaltation of the virtuous is the foundation of government?

厚葬久丧实不可以富贫众寡 〔50〕

Elaborate funerals and lengthy mourning cannot enrich the poor, and cannot increase the population.

J

俭节则昌，淫佚则亡 〔52〕

Frugality and economy bring prosperity, while indulgence and excess lead to demise.

江河不恶小谷之满己也，故能大 〔54〕

The large rivers do not despise the streams and brooks as tributaries.

江河之水，非一源之水也 〔56〕

The water in a river does not come from a single source.

今若有能以义名立于天下，以德来诸侯者 〔58〕

If there were someone who would establish his righteous name in the world and draw the feudal lords to him with his virtue ...

今唯无以厚葬久丧者为政 〔60〕

If those who take elaborate funerals and lengthy mourning as a principle of government are in office ...

今士之用身，不若商人之用一布之慎也 〔62〕

The officials of today deploy their power with even less discretion than the merchant would spend a coin.

今小为非，则知而非之。大为非攻国，则不知而非〔64〕

When a small wrong is committed people know that they should condemn it, but when such a great wrong as attacking a state is committed ...

今有人于此，少见黑曰黑，多见黑曰白〔66〕

If there were a man who, upon seeing a little blackness, will say it is black, but, upon seeing much, will say it is white ...

今用义为政于国家，国家必富〔68〕

If righteousness is employed in governing the state, the state will be rich.

近者不亲，无务来远〔70〕

When people nearby are not befriended, there is no use in endeavouring to befriend people who are distant.

君臣相爱，则惠忠〔72〕

When a ruler and his subordinates love each other, the ruler is gracious and the subordinates loyal.

君子不镜于水，而镜于人〔74〕

The superior man does not look to still water, but man, for his reflection.

君子战虽有陈，而勇为本焉〔76〕

The superior man may have strategies in war, but courage is

their fundamental value.

君子之道也，贫则见廉，富则见义〔78〕
The way of the superior man holds that he remains honest and
clean when in poverty, and righteous when wealthy.

君子自难而易彼，众人自易而难彼〔80〕
The superior man is strict with himself but lenient with others, while
the multitudes are lenient with themselves but strict with others.

L

吏不治则乱，农事缓则贫〔82〕
Slack governance will lead to disorder in the state, not attending
to agricultural activities will lead to poverty.

良弓难张，然可以及高入深〔84〕
Good bows may be hard to draw, but they reach great height
and depth.

M

民有三患〔86〕
The people worry about three things.

名不可简而成也，誉不可巧而立也〔88〕
The fame of the superior man is not obtained through arrogance and
pride, and his good reputation not through tricks and deception.

贫家而学富家之衣食多用，则速亡必矣〔90〕

If a poor family is to imitate the rich families in their extravagant clothes and food and other expenditures, ruin is very soon assured.

跂以为长，隐以为广〔92〕

It is like someone who stands on his tiptoes to appear tall, and lies down to appear broad.

去无用，之圣王之道〔94〕

To cut out what has no practical value is the way of the sage kings.

染于苍则苍，染于黄则黄〔96〕

What is dyed in blue becomes blue, what is dyed in yellow becomes yellow.

仁人事上竭忠，事亲得孝〔98〕

The magnanimous man in serving his sovereign should be loyal, and in waiting upon his parents should be filial.

仁之事者，必务求兴天下之利，除天下之害〔100〕

The magnanimous will pursue what benefits the world, and will abolish what is harmful.

仁者之为天下度也〔102〕

The magnanimous in their care for the people ...

入国而不存其士，则亡国矣〔104〕

When running the state, if the ruler does not care for the capable
and the virtuous, his state will be in danger.

若使天下兼相爱，国与国不相攻〔106〕

If people in the world love and care for one another, if states do
not attack one another ...

S

圣人为政一国，一国可倍也〔108〕

When a sage rules a state, the financial resources of the state
will be doubled.

圣人以治天下为事者也，必知乱之所自起〔110〕

The wise man who governs the state must know the cause of any
of its problems.

圣王为政，其发令兴事，使民用财也〔112〕

In issuing orders, launching undertakings, deploying his people,
and making use of the state's resources and wealth when the
sage king runs his state ...

施人薄而望人厚，则人唯恐其有赐于己也〔114〕

To give others little but to expect much from others would make them afraid of receiving any gift from the giver.

食必常饱，然后求美〔116〕
One will not mind whether the food is delicious and fine when
not being well fed.

世不渝而民不易，上变政而民改俗〔118〕
When the times do not alter, the people do not change, yet when
the government changes its regime the people will adapt to new
habits and customs.

世俗之君子，视义士不若视负粟者〔120〕
Uncultured people have even less regard for the righteous man
than for a grain carrier.

世俗之君子，皆知小物而不知大物〔122〕
Uncultured people understand only trifles, but not things of
importance.

世之君子，使之为一彘之宰，不能则辞之〔124〕
When being asked to be a butcher of pigs, uncultured people
would refuse if they know they are not capable.

视人之国若视其国，视人之家若视其家〔126〕
To regard the state of others as one's own, the houses of others
as one's own.

是故凡大国之所以不攻小国者〔128〕

The reason why a large state will not attack a small state is because ...

顺天意者，义政也〔130〕

To follow the will of Heaven is the righteous government of a state.

虽有贤君，不爱无功之臣〔132〕

The virtuous ruler does not favour ministers without merit.

所为贵良宝者，可以利民也〔134〕

Treasures are to be valued for they can benefit the people.

太上无败，其次败而有以成〔136〕

The best thing is to have no failure. The next best thing is to turn failure into success.

天地不昭昭，大水不潦潦〔138〕

Heaven and earth do not boast that they are bright and broad, great bodies of water do not boast that they are vast and boundless.

天下从事者，不可以无法仪〔140〕

To accomplish anything whatsoever one must have standards.

天下兼相爱则治，交相恶则乱〔142〕

When there is universal love in the world, the world will be peaceful, and when there is mutual hatred in the world, the world will be chaotic.

天下有义则生，无义则死〔144〕

11

With righteousness, the world thrives; without it, the world will meet its demise.

天下之百姓皆上同于天子，而不上同于天〔146〕

If the multitudes only obey the Son of Heaven but not the will of Heaven . . .

天下之人皆相爱，强不执弱，众不劫寡〔148〕

When all the people in the world love one another, the powerful will not control the vulnerable and the many will not loot the few.

天下之所以乱者，其说将何哉〔150〕

What is the reason for disorder in the world?

天下之所以生者，以先王之道教也〔152〕

The world survives because the teachings of the ancient virtuous kings are heeded.

天子为善，天能赏之〔154〕

When a ruler practicses virtue, Heaven rewards him.

天子者，天下之穷贵也，天下之穷富也〔156〕

The Son of Heaven is the most esteemed of the world and the wealthiest of the world.

天之行广而无私，其施厚而不德〔158〕

Heaven is all inclusive and impartial, and abundant in its blessings without asking for gratitude.

为义而不能，必无排其道〔160〕

When righteousness cannot be achieved, one must not complain about righteousness and abandon the way.

我有天志，譬若轮人之有规，匠人之有矩〔162〕

I understand the will of Heaven, like the wheelwright understands the compass, and the carpenter understands the square.

吾以为古之善者则述之，今之善者则作之〔164〕

I believe what was good in past times should be inherited and passed on. What is good in the present should also be carried on.

务言而缓行，虽辩必不听〔166〕

He who talks much but is slow in action will not be listened to, even though he is discerning.

兴天下之利，除天下之害〔168〕

Benefits for the people are promoted, harms for the world are eliminated.

言必立仪〔170〕

To express one's view, one needs to establish and adhere to

some standard.

言必有三表〔172〕

To express one's view, one needs to follow three principles.

言足以复行者，常之〔174〕

Doctrines proven feasible through practice over and again can be advocated.

言无务为多而务为智，无务为文而务为察〔176〕

In speech, it is not quantity but ingenuity, not eloquence but insight, that counts.

衣食者，人之生利也〔178〕

Clothing and food are the necessities of life.

以德就列，以官服事〔180〕

Ranks should be arranged according to virtue, tasks assigned according to office.

义者，善政也〔182〕

Governance with righteousness is good governance.

义者政也〔184〕

Righteousness means right and justifiable.

原浊者流不清，行不信者名必耗〔186〕

As a muddy source generates a stream not clear, unfaithful conduct tarnishes one's fame.

Z

谮慝之言，无入之耳〔188〕
Do not listen to any treacherous words.

争一言以相杀，是贵义于其身也〔190〕
One would rather die than give away righteousness. This shows
righteousness is even more valuable than one's life.

政者，口言之，身必行之〔192〕
To govern is to apply what one advocates to one's actions.

执无鬼而学祭礼，是犹无客而学客礼也〔194〕
To hold that there are no spirits, yet still learn sacrificial ceremonies
is similar to learning the etiquette of hospitality while having no guests.

志不强者智不达，言不信者行不果〔196〕
One's wisdom will not be far-reaching if his will is not strong.
One's action will not be resolute if he fails to keep his promises.

治于神者，众人不知其功〔198〕
The merit of the man who employs brilliant intelligence is not
recognized by the multitudes.

自古以及今，生民以来者，亦尝有见命之物〔200〕
From antiquity to the present, since the beginning of mankind,
has anyone seen such a thing as fate?

墨子说

MO ZI SAYS

墨子,姓墨名翟,春秋时鲁国人(一说宋国人或楚国人)。其生卒年月已不可详考,大约生活在孔子死后而孟子生前的时期。

墨子也曾以救世解纷为己任,授徒立说,周游列国,创立墨家学派。《韩非子·显学》:"世之显学,儒墨也。儒之所至,孔丘也。墨之所至,墨翟也。"由此形成和儒家并立的两大学派,当时"墨翟之言盈天下"(孟子语),可见其学派影响广大。

墨学的核心是"兼爱",即平等地爱一切人,由此而导致了他的"非攻"思想,反对一切攻伐战争。主张"节葬"、"非乐",对儒家倡导的繁文缛礼厚葬久丧主张加以反对,形成他的"非儒"思想。虽然如此,唐代儒学大师韩愈却有"孔子必用墨子,墨子必用孔子,不相用不足以为孔墨"之语,大有深意。

Master Mo, known in Chinese as Mo Zi, had a given name of Di. He was born in the State of Lu (or arguably in the State of Song or the State of Chu) in the Spring and Autumn Period (770 – 476 BC), in the period after Confucius' death and before Mencius' birth.

Mo Zi founded Mohism, one of the main philosophic schools in China. He had many followers, visited many states and gave lectures on his thoughts about governmental administration and the elimination of disorder and turmoil in society. Han Fei Zi, founder of the Logicians school, observed that "there are two famous schools of thought, one is Confucianism represented by Confucius, and the other is Mohism represented by Mo Di." Mohism was seen as a major rival to Confucianism, and had an extensive influence on society at that time. Mencius commented that, "Mo Di's words appear everywhere."

Mohism is best known for the concept of "universal love", that is, a person should care equally for other individuals, which consequently lead to his idea of "condemnation of offensive war". He was against any offensive war, and advocated "simplicity in funerals" and "condemnation of music". Unlike Confucius, Mo Zi spoke against the practice of extravagant burial rituals and long and lavish funerals, and this formed the basis of his "anti-Confucianism" thought. Yet despite their different beliefs, Han Yu, a renowned Confucian scholar in the Tang Dynasty insightfully noted that, "Confucianism borrows from Mohism, and Mohism borrows from Confucianism. The two schools become more complete upon learning from each other."

爱人利人，顺天之意

There are those who love the people and benefit the people and follow the will of Heaven.

老人家说系列丛书

墨子说

爱人利人，顺天之意，得天之赏者，有矣。憎人贼人，反天之意，得天之罚者，亦有矣。

《墨子·天志中》

There are those who love the people and benefit the people and follow the will of Heaven, and thus obtain reward from Heaven. There are also those who hate the people and harm the people and disobey the will of Heaven, and thus incur punishment from Heaven.

【注释】

墨子曰："夫爱人利人，顺天之意，得天之赏者，谁也？曰：若昔三代圣王尧舜禹汤文武者是也。……观其事，上利乎天，中利乎鬼，下利乎人。三利无所不利，是谓天德。""夫憎人贼人，反天之意，得天之罚者，谁也？曰：若昔三代暴王桀纣幽厉者是也。……观其事，上不利乎天，中不利乎鬼，下不利乎人。三不利无所不利，是谓天贼。"憎（zēng）：厌恶。《礼记·曲礼上》："爱而知其恶，憎而知其善。"贼（zé）：伤害。《孟子·梁惠王下》："贼仁者谓之贼，贼义者谓之残。"

【译文】

爱护人民，办事有利于百姓，施政顺从天意，因而受到上天奖赏的人是有的。厌恶人民，做事伤害百姓，施政违背天意，因而受到上天惩罚的人也是有的。

3

爱人利人者，天必福之

Those who love and benefit others will be blessed by Heaven.

爱人利人者，天必福之；恶人贼人者，天必祸之。

《墨子·法仪》

Those who love and benefit others will be blessed by Heaven. Those who hate and harm others will be punished by Heaven.

【注释】

墨子说："天必欲人之相爱相利，而不欲人之相恶相贼也。"因为天是兼爱的，即平等地爱一切人。所以"爱人利人以得福者有矣，恶人贼人以得祸者亦有矣"。贼：伤害。《孟子·梁惠王下》："贼仁者谓之贼，贼义者谓之残。"

【译文】

关爱别人、帮助别人的人，上天一定会赐福给他；憎恶别人、残害别人的人，上天一定会降祸给他。

备者，国之重也

For a state, preparations for what will occur are essential.

备者，国之重也；食者，国之宝也；兵者，国之爪也。

《墨子·七患》

For a state, preparations for what will occur are essential. Food stores are the treasure of a state, and armaments protect the state.

【注释】

备：储备。《尚书·说命中》："有备无患。"食：食物，粮食。《尚书·益稷》："暨稷播，奏庶艰食鲜食。"疏："与稷播种五谷，进于众人，难得食处，乃决水所得鱼鳖鲜肉为食也。"兵：兵器。《荀子·议兵》："古之兵，戈、矛、弓、矢而已矣。"爪（zhǎo）：本指鸟兽的脚，用以攻击和防卫。"国之爪也"，是说兵器是国家用来攻击和防卫的利器。

【译文】

储备是国家最重要的事，粮食是国家的宝物，武器是国家的利器。

本不固者末必几

Leaves and branches will wither if the roots are weak.

本不固者末必几，雄不修者其后必惰。

《墨子·修身》

Leaves and branches will wither if the root are weak. One will sink low if he does not improve and cultivate himself in his prime.

【注释】

几（jī）：危险。《左传·宣公十二年》："利人之几，而安人之乱。"注："几，危也。"雄：雄壮，雄强。《老子》第28章："知其雄，守其雌。"惰：衰败，堕落。

【译文】

根本不牢固枝叶必会枯萎，年轻时不修身后来必定会堕落。

不义不处，非理不行

What is not righteous and what is not reasonable should not be practised.

老人家说系列丛书

墨子说

不义不处，非理不行。务兴天下之利，曲直周旋，利则止，此君子之道也。

《墨子·非儒下》

What is not righteous and what is not reasonable should not be practised. One should endeavour to procure benefits for the state and persist in actions despite setbacks, avoiding that which brings no benefit. Such is the way of the superior man.

【注释】

不义：不应为的事。《左传·隐公元年》："多行不义，必自毙。" 曲直周旋：曲折反复。利则止：当作"不利则止"。也有注家说"止"应为"上"，上即尚贤之尚。言曲折周旋，唯利则尚也。墨家务兴天下之利，故尚利。此说似更近墨说。

【译文】

不行不义，不做不合理的事。务求兴办对天下有利的事，曲折反复也要去做，无利就停止，这才是君子处世的原则。

11

不义不富，不义不贵

The unrighteous shall not be granted wealth, the unrighteous shall not be honoured.

不义不富，不义不贵，不义不亲，不义不近。

《墨子·尚贤上》

The unrighteous shall not be granted wealth, the unrighteous shall not be honoured, the unrighteous shall not be trusted, the unrighteous shall not be favoured.

【注释】

这是墨子回答如何聚集贤良之士时引用古代圣王的话。他认为贤良之士是"国家之珍，社稷之佐"，所以对贤良之士要"富之、贵之、敬之、誉之"，这样国家的贤良之士就会多起来。**义**：仁义，正义。孔子以"义"作为评判人的思想行为的道德原则。"君子有勇而无义为乱，小人有勇而无义为盗"（《论语·阳货》）。**亲**：爱。《易·比》："先王以建万国，亲诸侯。"疏："亲诸侯，谓爵赏恩泽而亲友之。"作"亲近"解也可。《论语·学而》："泛爱众而亲仁。"**近**：接近，亲近。《尚书·五子之歌》："民可近，不可下。"

【译文】

不义的人不能让他富有，不义的人不能让他显贵，不义的人不能信任他，不义的人不能让他亲近。

仓无备粟，不可以待凶饥

Famine cannot be prepared against unless there are grains stored in the granaries.

仓无备粟，不可以待凶饥。库无备兵，虽有义，不能征无义。城郭不备完，不可以自守。心无备虑，不可以应卒。

《墨子·七患》

Famine cannot be prepared against unless there are grains stored in the granaries, and justice cannot be kept against the unjust unless there are ready weapons in the armoury. A city cannot be defended unless its inner and outer walls are in good repair, and emergencies cannot be met unless there have been plans of action made beforehand.

【注释】

墨子提出"备粟"、"备兵"、"备完"、"备虑"，教人以"备"防患于未然，有"备"无"患"。备：预备，准备。《尚书·说命中》："有备无患。"完：坚固。《孟子·离娄上》："城郭不完。"《荀子·议兵》："械用兵革攻完便利者强。"卒（cù）：同"猝"。急促。《战国策·燕策三》："群臣惊愕，卒起不意，尽失其度。"

【译文】

粮仓里没有储备粮食，就不能应付饥荒。武库里没有准备好兵器，即使正义在手也不能出兵攻击不义的军队。城郭防备不完善，就无法守卫。心无远虑，就不能应对突然变故。

藏于心者，无以竭爱

For the superior man, inside his heart there is endless love.

藏于心者，无以竭爱；动于身者，无以竭恭；出于口者，无以竭驯。

《墨子·修身》

For the superior man, inside his heart there is endless love, in his behaviour there is respectfulness, and from his mouth words are genteel.

【注释】

墨子是主张"兼爱"的，也就是平等地爱一切人。所以他说"藏于心者，无以竭爱"。竭爱：无尽的爱，普遍的爱。竭，穷尽。《礼记·曲礼上》："君子不尽人之欢，不竭人之忠。"《荀子·修身》："齐明而不竭，圣人也。"驯：雅驯，即典雅的意思。也可作"顺服"解。《列子·黄帝》："虽虎狼雕鹗之类，无不柔驯者。"

【译文】

（君子）深埋心中的，是无尽的爱；表现在行为上，是无比的谦恭，说出的话，是非常的典雅柔顺。

臣下重其爵位而不言，近臣则
喑，远臣则唫

If ministers value their positions and are afraid to speak their mind, whether near at hand or far away from the ruler, they will keep their silence.

墨子说

臣下重其爵位而不言，近臣则喑，远臣则喑，怨结于民心；谄谀在侧，善议障塞，则国危矣。

《墨子·亲士》

If ministers value their positions and are afraid to speak their mind, whether near at hand or far away from the ruler, they will keep their silence, and the people in turn will become bitter and unsatisfied. When the ruler is surrounded with flattery and insulated against good counsel, the state is in danger.

【注释】

墨子认为君主必须有敢于矫正自己过失的大臣，臣下则应以国是为重，敢于犯颜直谏而不应该过于看重自己的既得利益。故曰："归国宝，不若献贤而进士。"**近臣则喑，远臣则喑**：朝臣不言，远臣不议。近臣，君主左右亲近之臣。《仪礼·丧服》："众臣杖不以即位，近臣君服斯服矣。"喑（yīn），缄默，沉默不语。远臣，疏远之臣。一说指来自别国之臣。《孟子·万章上》："吾闻观近臣以其所为主，观远臣以其所主。"喑（jìn），闭口不言。**障塞**：阻隔。《礼记·月令》："开通道路，毋有障塞。"

【译文】

臣下如果过于看重自己的爵位而不敢进谏，近臣不言，远臣不议，不满情绪就会郁结于民心；谄媚阿谀之人围在君主身边，好的建议被阻塞，那国家就危险了。

大国之攻小国，譬犹童子之为马也

Large states attacking smaller ones are like boys riding on bamboo sticks as horses.

墨子说

大国之攻小国，譬犹童子之为马也。童子之为马，足用而劳。

《墨子·耕柱》

Large state attacking smaller ones are like boys riding on bamboo sticks as horses. When boys play the horse-riding game, they merely tire out their own feet.

【注释】

这是墨子对楚平王孙子（鲁阳文子）说的话。意思是大国攻打小国，就像儿童骑竹马一样，虽然骑在"马"上，还得自己双脚跑路。大国为进攻小国而劳民伤财，小国为防御大国进攻而劳民伤财，大国小国在这场兼并战争中其实是两败俱伤。这体现了墨子的"非攻"思想。**童子之为马：**童子骑竹马。竹马，儿童游戏时当"马"骑的竹竿。《文选》注引《幽求子》曰："年五岁间有鸠年之乐，七岁有竹马之欢。"《抱朴子·应嘲》："孺子之竹马，不免于脚剥。"剥，伤害。《后汉书·郭汲传》："始至行郡，到河西美稷，有童儿数百，各骑竹马，道次迎拜。"后人常用儿童骑竹马迎郭汲的故事称颂地方官吏。唐·白居易《赠楚州郭使君》诗："笑看儿童骑竹马，醉携宾客上仙舟。"

【译文】

大国攻打小国，就好像儿童骑竹马一样。虽然骑在"马"上，还得自己双脚跑路。

大国之攻小国也，是交相贼也

The attack by a large state on a small state injures both.

大国之攻小国也，是交相贼也，过必反于国。

《墨子·鲁问》

The attack by a large state on a small state injures both, and the consequences of the mistake will return to the large state.

【注释】

齐国将要进攻鲁国，墨子对齐国将领项子牛说："攻打鲁国，是齐国的大错。"他列举了历史上大国攻打小国反而自己受害的战例后说："大国攻打小国，是互相残害，大国的错误必定会反过来伤害自己。" **交相贼也**：互相残害。墨子认为大国为了攻打小国劳民伤财，小国为了应对大国的进攻也劳民伤财，所以是"交相贼也"。**过必反于国**：大国的错误必定反过来使本国受害。反，同"返"。

【译文】

大国攻打小国，那是互相残害，大国的错误必定反过来伤害自己。

得意，贤士不可不举；不得意，贤士不可不举

The virtuous must be exalted in peace and war.

墨子说

　　得意，贤士不可不举；不得意，贤士不可不举。尚欲祖述尧舜禹汤之道，将不可以不尚贤。夫尚贤者，政之本也。

《墨子·尚贤上》

　　The virtuous must be exalted in peace and war. If it is desired to continue the ways of Yao, Shun, Yu and Tang, the four sage kings, to exalt the virtuous is indispensable. Exaltation of the virtuous is the root of government.

【注释】

　　得意：因如愿以偿而感到满意。《韩非子·饰邪》："赵代先得意于燕，后得意于齐。"这里作国家太平解。治国如意故得意。**祖述**：师法前人，加以陈说。《礼记·中庸》："仲尼祖述尧舜，宪章文武。"**尚贤**：尊崇贤才。《易·大畜》："刚上而尚贤。"尚，尊崇。《论语·阳货》："君子尚勇乎！"**本**：事物的根基或主体。《论语·学而》："君子务本。"《商君书·更分》："法令者，民之命也，为治之本也，所以备民也。"

【译文】

　　国家太平，不可以不举荐贤才；国家不太平，不可以不举荐贤才。如果想要继承尧、舜、禹、汤圣王的治国之道，就不能不崇尚贤才。崇尚贤才，是治政的根本。

非无安居也，我无安心也

It is not that one has no comfortable abode but that one has no peaceful mind.

非无安居也，我无安心也；非无足财也，我无足心也。

《墨子·亲士》

It is not that one has no comfortable abode but that one has no peaceful mind; it is not that one has no sufficient wealth but that one yearns for more.

【注释】

安居：安宅，安定的居所。《诗经·小雅·鸿雁》："虽则劬劳，其究安宅？"安，安定，舒服。《诗经·小雅·谷风》："将恐将惧，维予与女。将安将乐，女转弃予。"《论语·学而》："君子食无求饱，居无求安。"《庄子·达生》："安时而处顺，哀乐不能入也。"安心：心安。足财：足够的财物。足，充实，足够，满足。《诗经·小雅·信南山》："既霑既足，生我百谷。"《论语·颜渊》："百姓足，君孰与不足？百姓不足，君孰与足？"这是孔子弟子有若回答鲁哀公所问"年饥，用不足。如之何"时所言，体现了儒家的民本思想。足心：心里满足，知足。《老子》第33章："知足者富。"

【译文】

不是没有安定的住处，是因为自己的心不安定；不是没有足够的财物，而是自己的心不知道满足。

夫义，天下之大器也

Righteousness is the greatest thing on earth.

老人家说系列丛书

夫义，天下之大器也，何以视人必强为之？

《墨子·公孟》

Righteousness is the greatest thing on earth. Why should one follow others in being righteous?

【注释】

有一个游学于墨子门下的人，墨子问："你为什么不学习呢？"那人回答说："我家族中没有人来学习。"于是墨子说了上面的话。**大器**：宝器。《左传·文公十二年》："君不忘先君之好，照临鲁国，镇抚其社稷，重之以大器，寡君敢辞玉。"注："大器，圭璋也。"

【译文】

墨子说："义，是天下最宝贵的东西，何必一定等别人先行呢？"

29

富贵者奢侈，孤寡者冻馁

The rich and high in rank are wasteful and extravagant, while the solitary and miserable are hungry and cold.

富贵者奢侈，孤寡者冻馁。虽欲无乱，不可得也。

《墨子·辞过》

The rich and high in rank are wasteful and extravagant, while the solitary and miserable are hungry and cold. It is impossible to keep such a society out of disorder.

【注释】

墨子认为执政者用财要节制，生活上要俭朴，这样人民才会富足，天下才会太平。**富贵：**多财曰富。《论语·学而》："贫而无谄，富而无骄。"位尊曰贵。《易·系辞上》："卑高以陈，贵贱位矣。"儒家重义轻富贵，孔子说："不义而富且贵，于我如浮云。"（《论语·述而》）**奢侈：**挥霍浪费。《国语·晋语》。"及桓子，骄泰奢侈，贪欲无艺。"**冻馁：**饥寒交迫。《墨子·非命上》："是以衣食之财不足，而饥寒冻馁之忧至。"

【译文】

富贵的人奢侈无度，孤寡之人受冻挨饿。执政者不想天下大乱，也是不可能的。

甘瓜苦蒂，天下物无全美

**The sweet melon has a bitter base near its stem.
Nothing is perfect in every way in the world.**

甘瓜苦蒂，天下物无全美。

《墨子佚文》

Sweet melon has a bitter base near its stem. Nothing is perfect in every way in the world.

【注释】

甘瓜苦蒂：甜瓜瓜蒂味苦。甘，甜。《诗经·邶风·谷风》："谁谓荼苦？其甘如荠。"荼（tú），指苦菜。荠（jì），指荠菜，味甜。**蒂**：花及瓜果与枝茎相连的部分。

【译文】

瓜甜蒂苦，天下没有十全十美的事物。

甘井近竭，招木近伐

The sweet wells become sooner exhausted and the tall trees are oftener felled.

甘井近竭，招木近伐，灵龟近灼，神蛇近暴。

《墨子·亲士》

The sweet wells become sooner exhausted and the tall trees are oftener felled. The tortoises that are more responsive are oftener burned to tell fortune, and the snakes that show more magic power are oftener dried in the sun to plead for rain.

【注释】

墨子说："有五把锥子，其中最锋利的一把会最先被用钝；有五块石头，其中一块是磨刀石，那么它会最先被磨损。"又说："比干死是因为他正直，孟贲被杀是因为他勇武，西施被沉江是因为她美丽，吴起被车裂是因为他能力太强。"所以说"太盛难守也"。**甘井近竭**：甜水井因取水的人多而先枯竭。近，先。《庄子·山木》："直木先伐，甘井先竭。"**招木**：乔木，高大的树木。**灵龟近灼**：灵龟，龟的一种。《尔雅·释鱼》："一曰神龟，二曰灵龟。"注："涪陵郡出大龟，甲可以卜，缘中文似玳瑁，俗呼为灵龟。"占卜时烧灼龟甲所见坼裂之纹以占吉凶，故说灵龟近灼。**神蛇近暴**：古代人常晒蛇祈雨。暴，同"曝"。

【译文】

甜水井最先枯竭，高大的树木最先被砍伐，灵龟最先被烧灼（占卜），神异的长蛇最先被曝晒（祈雨）。

古者圣王之政，列德而尚贤

In administering the government, the ancient sage kings ranked the morally excellent high and exalted the virtuous.

古者圣王之政，列德而尚贤。虽在农与工肆之人，有能则举之。

《墨子·尚贤上》

In administering the government, the ancient sage kings ranked the morally excellent high and exalted the virtuous. If capable, even a farmer or an artisan would be recruited and promoted.

【注释】

墨子尚贤，不仅选拔贤人，还要封以很高的爵位，给予丰厚的俸禄和决断的权力。**列德**：以德行授爵位。**工肆**：工人工作的作坊。工指工人，手工业劳动者。《论语·卫灵公》："工欲善其事，必先利其器。"肆，市集贸易之处。《论语·子张》："百工居肆，以成其事。"

【译文】

古代圣王治政，以德行授爵位，崇尚贤才。即使是农民和工匠中的人，只要有才能就会被选拔出来。

古者圣王甚尊尚贤而任使能

The ancient sage kings exalted the virtuous and promoted the capable.

古者圣王甚尊尚贤而任使能，不党父兄，不偏贵富，不嬖颜色。

《墨子·尚贤中》

The ancient sage kings exalted the virtuous and promoted the capable，without special consideration and favour for relatives，for the rich and honoured，or for the good-looking.

【注释】

尚贤使能：尊崇贤人，任用有才能的人。党：偏私。《尚书·洪范》："无偏无党，王道荡荡；无党无偏，王道平平。"偏：不公正，偏袒。《尚书·洪范》："无偏无陂。"嬖：宠爱。《左传·襄公二十五年》："叔孙还，纳其女于灵公，嬖，生景公。"《史记·周本纪》："幽王嬖爱褒姒。"

【译文】

古代圣明君主特别主张尚贤使能，不偏私亲人，不偏袒权贵，不亲近美色。

古之学者，得一善言附于其身

The learned men in the ancient times earnestly practised the good and wise advice they received.

墨子说

　　古之学者，得一善言附于其身；今之学者，得一善言务以说人，言过而行不及。

《墨子佚文》

　　The learned men in the ancient times earnestly practised the good and wise advice they received; the learned men in the current age teach others with the good and wise advice they received, as they talk more and do less.

【注释】

　　《书钞》引《新序》曰："齐王问墨子曰：古之学者为己，今之学者为人，何如？"墨子以上言对之。《论语·宪问》："子曰：'古之学者为己，今之学者为人。'"可见这一命题是当时国君问政或学者讲学常常说到的。**善言**：有益的话。《大戴礼记·子张问入官》："善言必听，详以失之。"意谓有益之言必采纳之。也指高妙之论为善言。《商君书·靳令》："法已定矣，不以善言害法。"**附**：增益。《荀子·礼论》："刻死而附生谓之墨，刻生而附死谓之惑。"**说**：劝说别人服从自己的意见。《孟子·尽心下》："说大人，则藐之，勿视其巍巍然。"

【译文】

　　古代学者，听到有益的话一定身体力行；现在的学者，听到有益的话则一定会用来教训别人，说得多而行动跟不上。

官无常贵，而民无终贱

Officials cannot be in constant honour, and ordinary people in eternal humbleness.

官无常贵，而民无终贱。有能则举之，无能则下之。

《墨子·尚贤上》

Officials cannot be in constant honour, and ordinary people in eternal humbleness. If a person is capable, promote him, if incapable, demote him.

【注释】

墨子要求选拔贤才要"举义不辟贫贱"、"举义不辟亲疏"、"举义不辟远近"、"举公义，辟私怨"。常：恒久，经常。《易·系辞上》："动静有常，刚柔断矣。"终：久常，永远。《论语·尧曰》："允执其中，四海困穷，天禄永终。"下：去，除。《周礼·秋官·司民》·"岁登下其死生。"注："下犹去也。每岁更著生去死。"

【译文】

官员并不能永远富贵，老百姓也不是一直贫贱。有能力就提拔他，不称职就罢免他。

国有贤良之士众，则国家之治厚

When the virtuous are numerous in the state, the foundation of the state is solid.

国有贤良之士众，则国家之治厚；贤良之士寡，则国家之治薄。

《墨子·尚贤上》

When the virtuous are numerous in the state, the foundation of the state is solid; when the virtuous are scarce, the foundation of the state is weak.

【注释】

尚贤是墨子的重要思想之一，他认为这是"为政之本"，他把对贤士的任用和国家的长治久安联系在一起。他认为执政者的主要任务就是聚集贤良之士。贤良之士多，国家治理的根基就坚实。**贤良**：有德行的人。《荀子·王制》："选贤良，举笃敬，兴孝弟，收孤寡，补贫穷，如是则庶人安政矣。"

【译文】

国家聚集的贤良之士多，治理国家的根基就坚实；国家聚集的贤良之士少，治理国家的根基就薄弱。

国之治也，治之，故治也

A country is politically stable, because it is well governed.

老人家说系列丛书

墨子说

国之治也，治之，故治也。治之废，则国之治亦废。国之富也，从事，故富也。从事废，则国之富亦废。

《墨子·公孟》

A country is politically stable, because it is well governed. As soon as good administration is abandoned, stability disappears also. A country is rich, because work is being attended to. As soon as work is abandoned, wealth disappears also.

【注释】

国之治也，治之，故治也：国家安定，是因为治理了，所以才会安定。国之治也，治与"乱"相对，特指政治清明安定。《易·系辞下》："黄帝尧舜垂衣裳而天下治。"治之，治，治理。《论语·宪问》："王孙贾治军旅。"故治也，治，安定。治之废，则国之治亦废：如果停止了治理，那国家的清明安定也就不存在了。治之废，废，停止。《老子》第18章："大道废，有仁义。"则国之治亦废，废，衰败，衰亡。《孟子·离娄上》："国之所以废兴存亡者亦然。"从事：办事，处理事务。《诗经·小雅·十月之交》："黾勉从事，不敢告劳。"黾（mǐn）勉，尽力，努力。

【译文】

国家政治安定，是因为努力治理了，所以才有安定的局面，如果停止了治理，那安定的局面也就不存在了。国家富裕，是因为努力生产了，所以才富裕，如果停止了生产，那么国家就不会富裕了。

何以知尚贤之为政本也

How do we know exaltation of the virtuous is the foundation of government?

何以知尚贤之为政本也？曰：自贵且智者为政乎愚且贱者则治，自愚且贱者为政乎贵且智者则乱，是以知尚贤之为政本也。

《墨子·尚贤中》

How do we know exaltation of the virtuous is the foundation of government? Master Mo said, when the honourable and wise run the government, the ignorant and humble remain orderly; but when the ignorant and humble run the government, the honourable and wise become rebellious. Therefore we know that exaltation of the virtuous is the foundation of good government.

【注释】

政本：治政之根本。贵且智：贤与能。贵，位尊。《易·系辞上》："卑高以陈，贵贱位矣。"智，才能。《国语·周语下》："言智必及事。"注："能处事物为智。"

【评文】

怎么知道尚贤为治政之本呢？（墨子）说：尚贤使能天下就太平，不尚贤使能天下就混乱，由此知道尚贤为治政之本也。

厚葬久丧实不可以富贫众寡

Elaborate funerals and lengthy mourning cannot enrich the poor, and cannot increase the population.

老人家说系列丛书

厚葬久丧实不可以富贫众寡，定危理乱乎，此非仁非义，非孝子之事也。

《墨子·节葬下》

Elaborate funerals and lengthy mourning cannot enrich the poor, cannot increase the population, and cannot remove the instability in a society; it is not magnanimous and righteous, nor is it the duty of a filial son.

【注释】

厚葬久丧：儒家讲究厚葬久丧，对不同地位和身份的人，在丧葬制度上要有所区别，比如天子之丧棺椁四重；守丧时间要达到规定的长度，如对父母行三年之丧，故称厚葬久丧。在墨子看来这都是毫无意义的浪费，厚葬久丧决不是圣王之道。定危理乱：转危为安，治理混乱。定，安定。《易·家人》："正家而天下定矣。"理乱，治理混乱。《魏书·高允传》："移风易俗，理乱解纷。"理，治理。

【译文】

厚葬久丧不能使贫困变得富裕，也不能使人口增加，不能使混乱的社会安定下来，这决不是仁，不是义，也不是孝子应该做的事。

俭节则昌，淫佚则亡

Frugality and economy bring prosperity, while indulgence and excess lead to demise.

俭节则昌，淫佚则亡。

《墨子·辞过》

Frugality and economy bring prosperity, while indulgence and excess lead to demise.

【注释】

墨子主张在宫室、衣服、饮食、舟车、蓄私五个方面要节俭，不可奢侈。昌（chāng）：兴盛、成长。《尚书·仲虺之诰》："推亡固存，邦乃其昌。"《荀子·礼论》："江河以流，万物以昌。"**淫佚**：谓纵欲放荡。《国语·周语上》："国之将亡，其君贪冒辟邪，淫佚荒怠。"淫，过度，过甚。《左传·襄公二十九年》："迁而不淫，复而不厌。"注："淫，过荡。"佚，安乐。通"逸"。

【译文】

节俭就会昌盛，奢侈就会灭亡。

江河不恶小谷之满己也，故能大

The large rivers do not despise the streams and brooks as tributaries.

江河不恶小谷之满己也，故能大。圣人者，事无辞也，物无违也，故能为天下器。

《墨子·亲士》

The large rivers do not despise the streams and brooks as tributaries. Great men do not shirk any tough task, or act counter to the innate laws of things, and so they become sage kings who reign the world.

【注释】

满·弃盈。《荀子·解蔽》："顷筐易满也。" **事无辞也，物无违也**：不推辞难事，不违背物理。辞，推辞不受。《论语·雍也》："与之粟九百，辞。"物，事物的内容实质。《易·家人》："君子以言有物，而行有恒。"违，违背。《孟子·梁惠王上》："不违农时，谷不可胜食也。"器：古代标志名位、爵号的器物。《左传·成公二年》："唯器与名，不可以假人。"

【译文】

长江黄河不嫌弃条条小溪流入，所以能汇成巨流。圣人不推辞难事，不违背物理，所以能成为治理天下的圣君。

江河之水，非一源之水也

The water in a river does not come from a single source.

老人家说系列丛书

墨子说

江河之水，非一源之水也；千镒
之裘，非一狐之白也。

《墨子·亲士》

The water in a river does not come from a single source,
neither is the fur coat of high value composed of the finest fur
of a single fox.

【注释】

墨子认为江河不弃小溪，故能汇成巨流。圣人不推辞难事，不违背物理，所以
能成为圣人。**千镒之裘**：价值千金的皮衣。镒（yì），古代重量单位。《孟子·公孙
丑下》："于宋，馈七十镒而受。"注："古者以一镒为一金，一镒是为二十四两也。"
裘（qiú），皮衣。《诗经·小雅·都人士》："彼都人士，狐裘黄黄。"**一狐之白**：中
国古代有集腋成裘的说法，狐狸腋下的毛纯白无杂，但一只狐狸只有很小的一块，
做成一件裘皮衣，需要很多只狐狸腋下的皮毛集合而成。

【译文】

长江黄河不止一个水源，价值千金的裘皮衣不是一
只狐狸腋下的毛皮所能做成的。

MO ZI SAYS

今若有能以义名立于天下，以德来
诸侯者

If there were someone who would establish his righteous name in the world and draw the feudal lords to him
with his virtue . . .

58

今若有能以义名立于天下，以德来诸侯者，天下之服可立而待也。

《墨子·非攻下》

If there were some one who would establish his righteous name in the world and draw the feudal lords to him with his virtue, the submission of the whole world would be offered to him immediately.

【注释】

墨子主张"非攻"，而当时好攻之君则百般粉饰攻伐战争说："我非以金玉子女壤地为不足也，我欲以义名立于天下，以德来诸侯也。"墨子说了上面的话。来：招致。《吕氏春秋·不侵》："不足以来士矣。"

【译文】

现在如果真有以道义的名义立于天下，以仁德招致诸侯来归的人，天下就会马上归服于他。

今唯无以厚葬久丧者为政

If those who take elaborate funerals and lengthy mourning as a principle of government are in office . . .

今唯无以厚葬久丧者为政，国家必贫，人民必寡，刑政必乱。

《墨子·节葬下》

If those who take elaborate funeral and lengthy mourning as a principle of government are in office, the state will become poor, the population grow less, and the jurisdiction disorderly.

【注释】

刑政：刑罚与政令。《荀子·王制》："刑政平，百姓和。"刑，处罚的总称。《尚书·大禹谟》："刑期于无刑。"政，政事，政令。《韩非子·五蠹》："今欲以先王之政，治当世之民，皆守株之类也。"《荀子·致士》："政令不行而上下怨疾，乱所以自作也。"

【译文】

现在如果让主张厚葬久丧的人来主政，国家必定贫困，人口必定会减少，刑政必定会混乱。

今士之用身，不若商人之用一布之
慎也

The officials of today deploy their power with even
less discretion than the merchant would spend a coin.

今士之用身，不若商人之用一布之慎也。

《墨子·贵义》

The officials of today deploy their power with even less
discretion than the merchant would spend a coin.

【注释】

墨子说："商人使用一枚钱都很谨慎，不肯轻易交易。而士人为官，却随意胡
行，重的受刑罚，轻的被人诟骂也不知悔改。"士：士人，士大夫。《宋书·恩幸传
论》："士子居朝，咸有职业。"《孟子·公孙丑下》："有士于此，而子悦之。"士，
一作"仕"。**用身**：以生命效力。用，效劳、出力。《商君书·靳令》："六虱成群，
则民不用。"身，自我，自身，生命。《论语·学而》："事君，能致其身。"致其身，
豁出生命。**布**：古代一种货币名称。《诗经·卫风·氓》："氓之蚩蚩，抱布贸丝。"
《周礼》郑注曰："布，泉也。其藏曰泉，其行曰布。"

【译文】

现在做官的人滥用职权，还不如商人使用一枚钱币
时谨慎。

今小为非，则知而非之。大为非攻
国，则不知而非

When a small wrong is committed people know that they should condemn it, but when such a great wrong as attacking a state is committed people do not know that they should condemn it.

今小为非，则知而非之。大为非攻国，则不知而非，从而誉之，谓之义。此可谓知义与不义之辩乎？

《墨子·非攻上》

When a small wrong is committed people know that they should condemn it, but when such a great wrong as attacking a state is committed people do not know that they should condemn it. On the contrary, it is acclaimed and called righteous. Is this deemed as able to tell the difference between the righteous and the unrighteous?

【注释】

小为非：指偷人桃李，窃人鸡狗猪，牵人牛马之类的过错。知而非之：知道这是错误的而谴责他。大为非攻国：墨子认为攻国是最大的不义。故说："今至大为不义攻国。"

【译文】

对人的小过错，大家都知道是错的，因而谴责它。但对攻伐别人国家这种大错误，大家却不认为是错的，反而赞美它，认为这是正义的行为。这能说是明白什么是义与不义的区别吗？

今有人于此，少见黑曰黑，多见黑曰白

If there were a man who, upon seeing a little blackness, will say it is black, but, upon seeing much, will say it is white ...

今有人于此，少见黑曰黑，多见
黑曰白，则以此人不知白黑之辩矣。

《墨子·非攻上》

If there is a man who, upon seeing a little blackness, will say it is black, but, upon seeing much, will say it is white, then we know that he cannot tell the difference between black and white.

【注释】

墨子还说了"少尝苦曰苦，多尝苦曰甘"的话。一人不诚信，大家知道这是不对的，当整个社会不诚信，就不会有人认为这是不对的了。墨子还说：有人到别人家果园里偷摘桃子、李了，大家都知道这是错误的行为，长官也会因此而惩罚他，因为这是损人利己的行为。但是国君率领军队去攻打别的国家，却没有人谴责他，反而认为这是正义的行为。墨子的"非攻"思想既指出攻国的残暴，又谴责维护战争的立场。

【译文】

现在这里有一个人，见到很少一点黑色就知道是黑色，但看见很多黑色却说是白色，于是人们都认为他是个黑白不分的人。

今用义为政于国家，国家必富

If righteousness is employed in governing the state, the state will be rich.

今用义为政于国家，国家必富，人民必众，刑政必治，社稷必安。

《墨子·耕柱》

If righteousness is employed in governing the state, the state will be rich, its population will grow, the administration will be in order, and the state's power will be secured.

【注释】

用义为政：用义来施行政治。墨子重义，说："天欲义而恶不义。"（《墨子·天志上》）又说，"义者政也。"意谓："义，就是匡正的意思。"刑政：刑罚与政令。《荀子·王制》："刑政平，百姓和。"社稷：土、谷之神。《周礼·春官·大宗伯》："以血祭祭社稷五祀五岳。"注："社稷，土谷之神，有德者配食焉。"《白虎通义·社稷》："人非土不立，非谷不食，……故封土立社，示有土也；谷，五谷之长，故立稷而祭之也。"后因以社稷作为国家政权的标志。《孟子·尽心下》："民为贵，社稷次之，君为轻。"

【译文】

现在用义来施政于国家，国家一定会富强，人口一定会增多，刑罚和政令一定会实行，政权一定会安定。

近者不亲，无务来远

When people nearby are not befriended, there is no use in endeavouring to befriend people who are distant.

墨子说

近者不亲，无务来远；亲戚不附，无务外交；事无终始，无务多业；举物而暗，无务博闻。

《墨子·修身》

When people nearby are not befriended, there is no use in endeavouring to befriend people who are distant; when relatives are not submissive, there is no use in endeavouring to socialize with others. When a person cannot accomplish a single task from start to finish, there is no use in attempting many tasks; when one is ignorant of a single matter, there is no use in pursuing wide knowledge.

【注释】

近者不亲，无务来远：身边的人不能亲近，就别希望招徕远方之人。《论语·子路》："叶公问政，子曰：'近者说，远者来。'"说，同"悦"。言近居之民以政治清明而欢悦，远方之民闻风而附。与此意近。后因以"近悦远来"指清明之政。附：归附，顺从。《淮南子·主术》："群臣亲，百姓附。"外交：与外（远）人交际。《史记·邓通传》："通亦愿谨，不好外交。"事无终始，无务多业：一件事不能善始善终，就不要贪做很多事。终，事物结局。与"始"相对。《易·系辞下》："易之为书也，原始原终。"业，事务，职业。《国语·周语上》："庶人工商，各守其业。"《荀子·王霸》："百亩一守，事业穷，无所移之也。"注："事业，耕稼也。"暗（àn）：不明白，不懂得。

【译文】

身边的人不能亲近，就别希望招徕远方之人；亲戚不能顺从，就不要对外交际；一事尚不能善始善终，就不要延揽各种事务；一事尚且不能明白，就不要追求广见博闻。

君臣相爱，则惠忠

When a ruler and his subordinates love each other, the ruler is gracious and the subordinates loyal.

君臣相爱，则惠忠；父子相爱，则慈孝；兄弟相爱，则和调。

《墨子·兼爱中》

When a ruler and his subordinates love each other, the ruler is gracious and the subordinates loyal; when a father and son love each other, the father is affectionate and the son filial; when elder and younger brothers love each other they are close and harmonious.

【注释】

惠忠：君主施恩惠于臣下，臣下效忠于君主。惠，恩惠。《国语·晋语四》："未报楚惠而抗宋，我曲楚直。"忠，忠诚。《荀子·大略》："比干子胥忠而君不用。"

慈孝：父母爱子女，子女孝顺父母。慈，爱。多指父母爱抚子女。《国语·吴语》："老其老，慈其幼，长其孤。"孝，旧时称善事父母为孝。《尚书·尧典》："克谐以孝。"和调：调和，和合，协调。《易·乾》："保合大和。"《荀子·修身》："血气刚强，则柔之调和。"

【译文】

君臣相爱，君惠臣忠；父子相爱，父慈子孝；兄弟相爱，兄友弟恭。

君子不镜于水，而镜于人

The superior man does not look to still water, but man, for his reflection.

君子不镜于水，而镜于人。镜于水见面之容，镜于人则知吉与凶。

《墨子·非攻中》

The superior man does not look to still water, but man, for his reflection. In water one sees only one's own face; in man one is able to foresee future good and bad.

【注释】

这是墨子引古人的话，故引文前有"古者有语曰"，后有"今以攻战为利，则盖尝鉴之于智伯之事乎"。《尚书·酒诰》："古人有言曰：'人无于水监，当于民监。'"《太公金匮阴谋》有武王《镜铭》："以镜自照见形容，以人自照见吉凶。"**镜于水**：以水为镜。镜，照。**吉凶**：吉，善，利。《逸周书·武顺》："礼义顺祥曰吉。"凶，不吉曰凶。《易·乾》："与鬼神合其吉凶。"

【译文】

君子不以水为镜，而以人为镜，以水为镜可以照见面容，以人为镜可以照见吉凶祸福。

君子战虽有陈，而勇为本焉

The superior man may have strategies in war, but courage is their fundamental value.

老人家说系列丛书

墨子说

君子战虽有陈，而勇为本焉；丧虽有礼，而哀为本焉；士虽有学，而行为本焉。

《墨子·修身》

The superior man may have strategies in war, but courage is their fundamental value; a funeral may have many rituals, but mourning and grief is its fundamental value; a scholar may have knowledge, but he must first of all exhibit good conduct.

【注释】

陈（zhèn）：战阵。同"阵"。《论语·卫灵公》："卫灵公问陈于孔子。"本：事物的根基或主体。《论语·学而》："君子务本。"《商君书·定分》："法令者，民之命也，为治之本也，所以备民也。"丧虽有礼，而哀为本焉：办丧事虽有一定的礼仪，但还是以哀痛为本。墨子主张节葬以反对儒家的厚葬久丧的丧葬制度。哀，悲伤，伤悼。《诗经·豳风·破斧》："哀我人斯，亦孔之将。"士：同"仕"。

【译文】

君子作战虽然讲究陈兵布阵，但还是以勇敢为本；办理丧事虽然有一定的礼仪制度，但还是以哀痛为本；做官虽然讲才学，但还是以品行为本。

君子之道也，贫则见廉，富则见义

The way of the superior man holds that he remains honest and clean when in poverty, and righteous when wealthy.

君子之道也，贫则见廉，富则见义，生则见爱，死则见哀，四行者不可虚假，反之身者也。

《墨子·修身》

The way of the superior man holds that he remains honest and clean when in poverty, and righteous when wealthy; he loves the living and mourns the dead. These four qualities of conduct cannot be hypocritically embodied, as they are nurtured through self-cultivation.

【注释】

墨子认为修身是"君子务本"的根本，而且他强调"反之身"的修养方法。"贫则见廉，富则见义，生则见爱，死则见哀"是他修身的主要内容。见（xiàn）：显露，出现。《论语·泰伯》："天下有道则见，无道则隐。"《战国策·燕策》："图穷而匕首见。"反之身：反省自身，这也是儒家修身的原则之一。《孟子·离娄上》："行有不得皆反求诸己，其身正而天下归之。"也作"反身"。《易·蹇》："君子以反身修德。"

【译文】

君子的处世原则是，贫穷时要廉洁，富贵时要重道义，爱护活着的人，哀悼死去的人。这四种行为不可弄虚作假，因为这是通过反省自身培养的品德。

君子自难而易彼，众人自易而难彼

The superior man is strict with himself but lenient with others, while the multitudes are lenient with themselves but strict with others.

君子自难而易彼，众人自易而难彼。

《墨子·亲士》

The superior man is strict with himself but lenient with others, while the multitude are lenient with themselves but strict with others.

【注释】

这是墨子对君子修养自身的主张，这和儒家的观点有相同之处。孔子曰："躬自厚，而薄责于人"（《论语·卫灵公》），西汉董仲舒对孔子这一思想又有所发挥："以仁治人，义治我，躬自厚而薄责于人，此之谓也"（《春秋繁露·仁义法》），《吕氏春秋·举难》："故君子责人则以仁，自责则以义。责人以仁则易足，易足则得人；自责以义则难为非，难为非则行饰。"朱熹《论语集注》："责己厚，故身益修；责人薄，故人易从，所以人不得而怨之。"**难**：责难。《孟子·离娄下》："君子曰：'此亦妄人也已矣。如此，则与禽兽奚择哉？与禽兽又何难焉？'"**易**：容易，与"难"相对。**众人**：大众，一般人。《论语·卫灵公》："众恶之，必察焉；众好之，必察焉。"

【译文】

君子严于律己宽于待人，一般人则是对己宽对人严。

吏不治则乱，农事缓则贫

Slack governance will lead to disorder in the state, not attending to agricultural activities will lead to poverty.

吏不治则乱，农事缓则贫，贫且乱政之本。

《墨子·非儒下》

Slack governance will lead to disorder in the state, not attending to agricultural activities will lead to poverty, and poverty is the root of political disorder and instability.

【注释】

儒家主张"天命论"曰："寿夭贫富，安危治乱，固有天命，不可损益。穷达赏罚幸否有极，人之知力，不能为焉。"墨子对此持批判态度说："官吏们听信儒家的天命论，就会懈怠自己的职责，老百姓听信了它，就会荒废农业生产。官吏不治理政事国家就会混乱，荒废了农业生产国家就会贫穷，贫穷是政治混乱的根源。"**缓**（huǎn）：迟缓，延误。《孟子·滕文公上》："民事不可缓也。"**乱政**：败坏政治。《左传·隐公五年》："乱政亟行，所以败也。"**本**：事物根基或主体。《论语·学而》："君子务本。"《商君书·定分》："法令者，民之命也，为治之本也，所以备民也。"

【译文】

官吏不治理政事国家就会混乱，荒废了农业生产国家就会贫穷，贫穷是政治混乱的根源。

良弓难张，然可以及高入深

Good bows may be hard to draw, but they reach great height and depth.

良弓难张，然可以及高入深；良马难乘，然可以任重致远；良才难令，然可以致君见尊。

《墨子·亲士》

Good bows may be hard to draw, but they reach great height and depth. Fine horses may be hard to ride, but they carry heavy loads and make long journeys. People of real talent may be hard to deploy, but they can shoulder great responsibilities for the state.

【注释】

良弓难张：硬弓难以拉开。良弓，好弓。《荀子·性恶》："繁弱钜黍，古之良弓也。"繁弱、钜黍，皆良弓名。《史记·淮阴侯列传》："高鸟尽，良弓藏。"张，拉紧弓弦，开弓。《诗经·小雅·吉日》："既张我弓，既挟我矢。"乘（chéng）：坐，驾。《诗经·邶风·二子乘舟》："二子乘舟，泛泛其景。"任重致远：负载重而路途远。《韩非子·人主》："夫马之所以能任重引本致远道者，以筋力也。"令：命令。《诗经·齐风·东方未明》："倒之颠之，自公令之。"致君见尊：使君主受到尊敬，言称霸之事。

【译文】

好弓难以拉开，但可以射得高远深厚；好马难以驾驭，但可以载重行远；杰出的人才难以调遣，但却能安邦治国。

民有三患

The people worry about three things.

民有三患：饥者不得食，寒者不得衣，劳者不得息。三者，民之巨患也。

《墨子·非乐上》

The people worry about three things: that the hungry cannot be fed, the cold cannot be clothed, and the tired cannot get rest. These three are the biggest worries of the people.

【注释】

墨子认为靠音乐歌舞是不能解决百姓吃饭穿衣问题的，也以此作为他"非乐"观点的论据之一。患：灾祸，忧患。《尚书·说命中》："惟事事乃其有备，有备无患。"《荀子·富国》："使百姓无冻馁之患，则是圣君贤相之事也。"劳：用力辛勤。《易·兑》："说以先民，民忘其劳。"

【译文】

百姓有三种忧患：饥饿的人得不到食物，受冻的人得不到衣服，劳累的人得不到休息。这三种情况，是百姓最大的忧患。

名不可简而成也，誉不可巧而立也

The fame of the superior man is not obtained through arrogance and pride, and his good reputation not through tricks and deception.

名不可简而成也，誉不可巧而立也。君子以身戴行者也。

《墨子·修身》

The fame of the superior man is not obtained through arrogance and pride, and his good reputation not through tricks and deception. The superior man cultivates himself through good practices.

【注释】

简：倨傲，怠慢。《吕氏春秋·骄恣》：“自骄则简士。”注：“简，傲也。”《孟子·离娄下》：“右师（王驩）不悦，曰：‘诸君子皆与驩言，孟子独不与驩言，是简驩也。’”巧：虚伪不实。《老子》第19章：“绝巧弃利，盗贼无有。”转作欺骗。《淮南子·本经》：“饰智以惊愚，设诈以巧上。”注：“巧，欺也。”戴：同“载”。

【译文】

君子的名声不会因傲慢而获得，荣誉不会因欺骗而建立。君子是以身体力行来修养自身的。

贫家而学富家之衣食多用，则速亡必矣

If a poor family is to imitate the rich families in their extravagant clothes and food and other expenditures, ruin is very soon assured.

贫家而学富家之衣食多用，则速亡必矣。

《墨子·贵义》

If a poor family is to imitate the rich families in their extravagant clothes and food and other expenditures, ruin is very soon assured.

【注释】

墨子对卫国大夫公良桓子说："卫国是个小国，地处齐国和晋国之间，就像贫穷之家处在富贵之家之间一样。贫家如果要仿效富家的穿衣吃饭一样讲究，还要应付巨大花费，便会因财力不支而加速灭亡。"这是墨子看到公良桓子家豪华奢侈无度，才这样说的。他认为与其学大国讲排场、比阔气，不如拿这些钱"养士"，尚能保国家安全。

【译文】

贫穷之家如果一味仿效富贵之家那样穿衣吃饭以及支持庞大的花费，就会很快招致灭亡。

跂以为长，隐以为广

It is like someone who stands on his tiptoes to appear tall, and lies down to appear broad.

跂以为长，隐以为广，不可久也。

《墨子·公孟》

It is like someone who stands on his tiptoes to appear tall, and lies down to appear broad. That is not true.

【注释】

有几个弟子对墨子说："告子能行仁义之事。"墨子说了上面的话，表示不相信告子能行仁义之事。跂（qǐ）：踮起脚尖。《史记·高祖记》："军吏士卒皆山东之人也，日夜跂而望归。"跂，通"企"。《老子》第24章："企者不立，跨者不行。"唐宋诸本《老子》"企"皆作"跂"。"跂"为"企"之假。隐：同"偃"。

【译文】

踮起脚尖以为自己长高了，卧倒在地以为自己面积大了，其实这并不是真相。

去无用，之圣王之道

To cut out what has no practical value is the way of the sage kings.

去无用，之圣王之道，天下之大利也。

《墨子·节用上》

To cut out what has no practical value is the way of the sage kings and a great benefit to all the people.

【注释】

去无用："去无用"是墨子"节用"的主要思想。意即去掉没有实用价值的东西。例如打造车船的原则是让它更加轻捷便利，只是为漂亮而增加的装饰部分都是"无用"的。去，除去，抛弃。《尚书·大禹谟》："去邪勿疑。"**利**：利益，功用。《商君书·算地》："利出于地，则民尽力。"《战国策·秦策一》："大王之国，西有巴蜀汉中之利。"

【译文】

去掉没有实用价值的东西，实行圣王的治国之道，这就是天下百姓最大的利益。

染于苍则苍，染于黄则黄

What is dyed in blue becomes blue, what is dyed in yellow becomes yellow.

墨子说

染于苍则苍，染于黄则黄。所入者变，其色亦变……非独染丝然也，国亦有染。

《墨子·所染》

What is dyed in blue becomes blue, what is dyed in yellow becomes yellow. When the silk is put in a different dye, its colour changes ... This is true not only with silk, for even a country changes with the influence it receives.

【注释】

墨子从染丝这件普通的事中提出了深刻的哲学内涵。墨子举舜被许由、伯阳所染，禹被皋陶、伯益所染，汤被伊尹、仲虺所染，周武王被姜太公、周公旦所染。这四个帝王，受到的熏染是得当的，所以能称王于天下，被立为天子，功业和名声覆盖大地。**染于苍则苍**：丝被青色一染就成了青色。染（rǎn），使布帛等物着色。也作"沾染、感受、影响"解。《吕氏春秋·当染》："舜染于许由、伯阳，禹染于皋陶、伯益。"苍，草色，引申为青黑色。**国亦有染**：治理国家也像染丝一样。

【译文】

丝被青色一染就成了青色，被黄色一染就成了黄色。染缸里的颜料变了，染出的丝的颜色也就变了……不光染丝如此，治理国家也是如此。

仁人事上竭忠，事亲得孝

The magnanimous man in serving his sovereign should be loyal, and in waiting upon his parents should be filial.

仁人事上竭忠，事亲得孝，务善则美，有过则谏，此为人臣之道也。

《墨子·非儒下》

The magnanimous man in serving his sovereign should be loyal, and in waiting upon his parents should be filial. When there is excellence in his sovereign he should give praise, when there is fault he should give counsel. This is the way of a minister.

【注释】

儒家说：“君子若钟，击之则鸣，弗击不鸣。”意思是说君子立于朝，君主发问就讲话，不问就不讲话。墨子反对这一观点，就说了上面的话后又说：以这种态度为人臣则不忠，为人子则不孝，对兄长就是不恭顺，对朋友就是不坦诚。**事上竭忠**：侍奉君主应当尽忠。事，侍奉。《易·蛊》：“不事王侯。”《荀子·王制》：“能以事亲谓之孝，能以事兄谓之弟。”竭（jié），穷尽。《礼记·曲礼上》：“君子不尽人之欢，不竭人之忠。”**事亲得孝**：侍奉父母应当尽孝。得，能。《韩诗外传》二：“不能勤苦，焉得行此。”如果把“得”作“获得”解，也通。

【译文】

仁义之人侍奉君主应当尽忠，侍奉父母应当尽孝，看到君主做得好的就称赞，有过失就劝谏，这才是做臣下的原则。

仁之事者，必务求兴天下之利，除
天下之害

The magnanimous will pursue what benefits the
world, and will abolish what is harmful.

墨子说

仁之事者，必务求兴天下之利，除天下之害。将以为法乎天下：利人乎，即为；不利人乎，即止。

《墨子·非乐上》

The magnanimous will pursue what benefits the world, and will abolish what is harmful. As a universal principle, what is beneficial to the people will be done, and what is not, will not be done.

【注释】

墨子"非乐"的观点是和儒家的"礼乐"主张相对立的。但他非乐的原因，是当时社会上王公大人们对于声乐的过分追求造成了"亏夺民衣食之财"的后果。**仁之事者**：当作"仁人之事者"。**法**：标准模式。《管子·七法》："尺寸也、绳墨也、规矩也、衡石也、斗斛也、角量也，谓之法。"《墨子·辞过》："故圣王作为宫室，为宫室之法。"

【译文】

仁义之人做事，必定要为天下人兴利除害。以此作为天下的准则：有利于人民的事，就做；不利于人民的事，就不做。

101

仁者之为天下度也

The magnanimous in their care for the people . . .

墨子说

仁者之为天下度也，非为其目之所美，耳之所乐，口之所甘，身体之所安。以此亏夺民衣食之财，仁者弗为也。

《墨子·非乐上》

The magnanimous in their care for the people do not think of doing things to delight their eyes, to please their ears, to gratify their appetite or to ease their body. The magnanimous would not undertake anything that deprives the people of their means of living.

【注释】

度（duó）：揣测，考虑。《诗经·小雅·巧言》："他人有心，予忖度之。"**目之所美**：看上去很悦目。美，美色。《诗经·邶风·静女》："匪女之为美，美人之贻。"**耳之所乐**：听起来很动人。乐（lè），喜悦。《诗经·小雅·常棣》："宜尔家室，乐尔妻帑。"**口之所甘**：吃起来香甜。甘，味美，甜。《尚书·洪范》："稼穑作甘。"注："甘味生于百谷。"**安**：逸乐，安逸。《左传·僖公二十三年》："怀与安，实败名。"**亏夺**：豪夺。亏，毁坏，灭损。《诗经·鲁颂·閟宫》："不亏不崩，不震不腾。"《易·谦》："天道亏盈而益谦。"

【译文】

仁义的人做事是要为天下百姓考虑的，并非为了自己耳目口体的逸乐享受，如果仅仅为了满足自己的这些私欲而豪夺天下百姓的衣食之资，（这种事）仁义的人是不会去做的。

入国而不存其士，则亡国矣

When running the state, if the ruler does not care for the capable and the virtuous, his state will be in danger.

入国而不存其士，则亡国矣。见贤而不急，则缓其君矣。非贤无急，非士无与虑国。缓贤忘士，而能以其国存者，未曾有也。

《墨子·亲士》

When running the state, if the ruler does not care for the capable and the virtuous, his state will be in danger. If the capable and the virtuous are not properly used, they will show indifference to their ruler. Deploying the capable and the virtuous is of the highest urgency, for they are the ones with strategies and plans for the state. No state will be able to maintain long-lasting stability if the capable and the virtuous are treated slightingly.

【注释】

墨子认为一个国家兴盛与衰亡的关键在于能否任用贤才。"亲士"的意思就是说要重视人才。**入国而不存其士**：治理国家而不关心贤士。入国，国内。《孟子·告子下》："入则无法家拂士，出则无敌国外患者，国恒亡。"赵岐注："入，谓国内也；出，谓国外也。"**缓贤忘士**：怠慢贤士，轻视人才。缓，迟缓，延缓。《孟子·滕文公上》："民事不可缓也。"

【译文】

治理国家却不关心贤士，就有亡国的危险。见到贤士而不能马上任用，他们就会对君主怠慢。没有什么事比选用贤士更急迫的，没有贤士就没有人谋划国家大事。怠慢贤士、轻视人才而能使国家长治久安，是从来没有的事。

若使天下兼相爱，国与国不相攻

If people in the world love and care for one another, if states do not attack one another . . .

若使天下兼相爱，国与国不相攻，家与家不相乱，盗贼无有，君臣父子皆能孝慈，若此则天下治。

《墨子·兼爱上》

If people in the world love and care for one another, if states do not attack one another and state officials do not plunder loot from other states, then thieves and robbers will become extinct. If rulers and ministers love each other, the rulers will be gracious, the ministers loyal. If fathers and sons love each other, fathers will be affectionate and sons filial, and the world will be in peace and order.

【注释】

国与国不相攻：诸侯国之间不相互攻伐。国，国家，诸侯国。《周礼·天官·太宰》："以佐王治邦国。"注："大曰邦，小曰国。"家：卿大夫的采地食邑。《周礼·夏官·序官》："家司马各使其臣。"注："家，卿大夫采地。"乱：掠夺。

【译文】

如果天下人能互相友爱，诸侯之间互不攻伐，大夫之间互不掠夺，盗贼就不会产生。君臣相爱，君惠臣忠；父子相爱，父慈子孝。如果这样天下就太平无事了。

圣人为政一国，一国可倍也

When a sage rules a state, the financial resources of the state will be doubled.

圣人为政一国，一国可倍也。大之为政天下，天下可倍也。其倍之，非外取地也。因其国家，去其无用，足以倍之。

《墨子·节用上》

When the wise man rules a state, the financial resources of the state will be doubled. When the wise man rules the world, the financial resources of the world will be doubled. The gain is not the result of acquiring the land of other states, but from cutting out extravagances and wastes in line with the state's situation.

【注释】

圣人：人格品德最高的人。《易·乾·文言》："圣人作而万物睹。"《老子》第22章："是以圣人抱一而天下式。"儒家典籍中多泛指尧舜禹汤文武周公孔子为圣人。自儒家一尊后，特指孔子为圣人。墨子所指应为尧舜禹汤。《墨子·尚贤上》："尚欲祖述尧舜禹汤之道，将不可以不尚贤。"无用：无益于实用的东西。"去无用"是墨子"节用"的主要办法。《墨子·节用上》："去无用，之圣王之道，天下之大利也。"例如，做衣服的原则就是冬天御寒、夏天防暑而已，只为漂亮加上去的装饰都是"无用"之物。

【译文】

圣人治理一个国家，一个国家的财力可以增加一倍。如果扩大到治理天下，天下的财力可以增加一倍，这增加的一倍财力不是靠向外掠夺土地得来的，只要根据国家的具体情况，去掉没有实用价值的浪费就足够了。

圣人以治天下为事者也，必知乱之
所自起

The wise man who governs the state must know the
cause of any of its problems.

圣人以治天下为事者也，必知乱之所自起，焉能治之；不知乱之所自起，则不能治。

《墨子·兼爱上》

The wise man who governs the state must know the cause of any of its problems before he can put them in order; he cannot handle the problem unless he knows its cause.

【注释】

墨子说：圣人治理天下就像医生为人看病一样，一定先查出病人的病根，然后才能对症下药。**焉**：乃。

【译文】

圣人治理天下的原则是一定要知道动乱发生的根源，才能治理；如果不知道动乱的根源，就不能治理。

圣王为政，其发令兴事，使民用
财也

In issuing orders, launching undertakings, deploying his people, and making use of the state's resources
and wealth when the sage king runs his state . . .

圣王为政，其发令兴事，使民用财也，无不加用而为者，是故用财不费，民德不劳，其兴利多矣。

《墨子·节用上》

In issuing orders, launching undertakings, deploying his people, and making use of the state's resources and wealth when running the state, the sage king never does anything without a useful purpose or without practicality. Therefore wealth is not wasted and people are not exhausted, yet notable benefits are generated.

【注释】

兴（xīng）：兴起，兴办。《礼记·乐记》："明于天地，然后能兴礼乐也。"无不加用而为者：无一不是有益于实用才去做的。加用，增加其用处。加，增加。《左传·隐公五年》："叔父有憾于寡人，寡人弗敢忘，葬之加一等。"德：同"得"。《孟子·告子上》："为宫室之美，妻妾之奉，所识穷乏者得我与？"得，同"德"。

【译文】

圣王治理国家，他发布政令，兴办事业，役使民众，使用财物，无一不是只讲究实用的，所以用财省，民不劳苦而得利多。

施人薄而望人厚，则人唯恐其有赐于己也

To give others little but to expect much from others would make them afraid of receiving any gift from the giver.

施人薄而望人厚，则人唯恐其有赐于己也。

《墨子·鲁问》

To give others little but to expect much from others would make them afraid of receiving any gift from the giver.

【注释】

鲁国负责祭祀的官员用一头小猪祭祀，向鬼神祈求百福。墨子认为这是送出去得少而希望回报得多，是不可以的。施：给予。《国语·吴语》："施民所欲，去民所恶。"望：盼望，希望。《荀子·天论》："望时而待之，孰与应时而使之。"《史记·黥布传》："布又大喜过望。"

【译文】

如果送给别人很少的东西却希望别人回报很多的东西，那人们就会怕你再送给他们东西了。

食必常饱，然后求美

One will not mind whether the food is delicious and fine when not being well fed.

墨子说

食必常饱，然后求美；衣必常暖，然后求丽；居必常安，然后求乐。

《墨子佚文》

One will not mind whether the food is delicious and fine when not being well fed, whether the clothing is luxurious and beautiful when not being well clad, and he will not seek for pleasure when he has no stable abode.

【注释】

食必常饱，然后求美：常年都能吃饱肚子，然后才要求美味。食，吃。《论语·学而》："君子食无求饱，居无求安。"美，美味。《韩非子·扬权》："夫香美脆味，厚酒肥肉，甘口而病形。"丽，华丽。乐：泛指声色。《国语·越语下》："今吴王淫于乐，而忘其百姓。"《墨子佚文》："乐者，圣王之所非也，而儒者为之，过也。"

【译文】

常年都能吃饱肚子，然后才要求美味；一年到头有衣服穿，然后才要求华丽；居住安定，然后才追求安乐。

世不渝而民不易，上变政而民改俗

When the times do not alter, the people do not change, yet when the government changes its regime the people will adapt to new habits and customs.

世不渝而民不易，上变政而民改俗。

《墨子·非命下》

When the times do not alter, the people do not change, yet when the government changes its regime the people will adapt to new habits and customs.

【注释】

墨子曰："昔者三代圣王禹汤文武方为政乎天下之时，曰：'必务举孝子而劝之事亲，尊贤良之人而教之为善。'是故出政施教，赏善罚暴。且以为若此，则天下之乱也，将属可得而治也；社稷之危也，将属可得而定也。若以为不然，昔桀之所乱，汤治之；纣之所乱，武王治之。"渝：变更。《诗经·郑风·羔裘》："彼其之子，舍命不渝。"易：改变。《易·系辞下》："上古结绳而治，后世圣人易之以书契。"俗：习俗，风气。《尚书·君陈》："败常乱俗。"《史记·李斯传》："孝公用商鞅之法，移风易俗。"

【译文】

世道不改，人民不变；君主变政，人民易俗。

世俗之君子，视义士不若视负粟者

Uncultured people have even less regard for the righteous man than for a grain carrier.

墨子说

世俗之君子，视义士不若视负粟者。今有人于此，负粟息于路侧，欲起而不能，君子见之，无长少贵贱，必起之。何故也？曰：义也。

《墨子·贵义》

Uncultured people have even less regard for the righteous man than for a grain carrier. If a carrier was resting by the road side and was unable to stand up, upon seeing him, a person, whether old or young, honourable or humble, would surely help him rise. Why? The person's answer would be: because it is righteous.

【注释】

义士：有节操的人。《左传·桓公二年》："武王克商，迁九鼎于雒邑，义士犹或非之。"墨子这里指行义的人为义士。义士奉行传承先王的道义而并不被世俗之君子们认同，反而遭非议诋毁。**负粟者**：背粮食的人。负，以背载物。《孟子·梁惠王上》："颁白者不负载于道路矣。"粟，粮食的通称。

【译文】

世俗之人对待行义之士还不如对待一个背粮食的人。现在有一个背粮食的人，坐在路边休息，想起来却起不来，别人看见了，不论老少贵贱，都会上前帮这个人站起来。这是为什么呢？回答说：这是义。

世俗之君子，皆知小物而不知大物

Uncultured people understand only trifles, but not things of importance.

世俗之君子，皆知小物而不知大物。今有人于此，窃一犬一彘，则谓之不仁；窃一国一都，则以为义。

《墨子·鲁问》

Uncultured people understand only trifles, but not things of importance. If a man steals a dog or a pig, they deem him wrong, but they regard the invasion of a state or attack of a city as righteous.

【注释】

物：事物。《诗经·大雅·烝民》："天生烝民，有物有则。"彘（zhì）：猪。《孟子·尽心上》："五母鸡，二母彘。"

【译文】

世俗之人只明白小事，却不明白大事。有人偷了一只狗一头猪，他们知道这是不仁的事；而侵略一个国家攻下一座城池，他们却认为这是行义。

世之君子，使之为一彘之宰，不能
则辞之

When being asked to be a butcher of pigs, uncultured people would refuse if they know they are not capable.

世之君子，使之为一彘之宰，不能则辞之；使为一国之相，不能而为之，岂不悖哉！

《墨子·贵义》

When being asked to be a butcher of pigs, uncultured people would refuse if they know they are not capable; they would anyhow accept an offer of being the Prime Minister of a state, though they know they are not capable. Isn't it ridiculous?

【注释】

一彘之宰：一个杀猪的屠夫。一国之相：一国的宰相。相，古官名。后专指宰相。《吕氏春秋·举难》："相也者，百官之长也。"悖（bèi），荒谬。

【译文】

世俗的人，让他做一个杀猪的屠夫，如果不能胜任便会推辞；让他做一国的宰相，纵然不能胜任他也不会辞职，这不是很荒谬吗？

视人之国若视其国，视人之家若视其家

To regard the state of others as one's own, the houses of others as one's own.

视人之国若视其国，视人之家若视其家，视人之身若视其身。是故诸侯相爱，则不野战；家主相爱，则不相篡；人与人相爱，则不相贼。

《墨子·兼爱中》

If it was that people regarded the state of others as one's own, the houses of others as one's own, the life of others as one's own, then feudal lords would love one another, and there would be no more war; heads of houses would love one another, and there would be no more plunder; individuals would love one another, there would be no more injury.

【注释】

国：诸侯国。《周礼·天官·太宰》："以佐王治邦国。"注："大曰邦，小曰国。"**家**：卿大夫的采地食邑。《周礼·夏官·序言》："家司马各使其臣。"注："家，卿大夫采地。"**身**：生命。**野战**：交战于旷野。《墨子·兼爱中》："诸侯不相爱，则必野战。"**篡**：用强力夺取。

【译文】

看待别人的国家就像看待自己的国家一样，看待别人的家园就像看待自己的家园一样，看待别人的生命就像看待自己的生命一样。这样的话，诸侯相爱，就不会发生攻伐战事；家主相爱，就不会互相掠夺；人与人相爱，就不会互相残害。

是故凡大国之所以不攻小国者

The reason why a large state will not attack a small state is because . . .

是故凡大国之所以不攻小国者，积委多，城郭修，上下调和，是故大国不耆攻之。

《墨子·节葬下》

The reason why a large state will not attack a small state is because the small state is well stocked with food supplies, its inner and outer city walls are in good repair, and its ruler and his people are unified. That is why a large state will not attack a small state.

【注释】

关于小国如何应对大国的兼并，孟子有和墨子相同的主张。有一次滕文公问孟子："滕国是一个小国，处在齐、楚这样的大国之间，我们是投靠齐国呢，还是投靠楚国呢？"孟子说："把护城河挖深，把城墙加固，和老百姓一道来保卫它，宁肯献出生命，也不放弃，那就有办法了。"**积委**：积聚，储备。也作"委积"。《周礼·地官·遗人》："掌邦之委积，以待施惠。"注："少曰委，多曰积。"**城郭**：内城与外城，泛指城邑。《管子·度地》："内为之城，外为之郭。"**调和**：和合，和谐。**耆**（zhǐ）：致。《诗经·周颂·武》："胜殷遏刘，耆定尔攻。"《国语·晋语》："及臣之壮也，耆其股肱以从司马，苛慝不产。"

【译文】

大国之所以不能兼并小国，必定是因为这个小国粮食储备充足，城郭修筑坚固，上下齐心协力，大国才不敢攻打它。

顺天意者，义政也

To follow the will of Heaven is the righteous government of a state.

顺天意者，义政也；反天意者，力政也。

《墨子·天志上》

To follow the will of Heaven is the righteous government of a state, to oppose the will of Heaven is the government of a state by force and power.

【注释】

义政：以义服人的政治。义，宜，适宜。合理、适宜的事称义。《易·乾》："利物足以合义，贞固足以干事。"疏："言天能利益庶物，使物各得其宜。"《论语·公冶长》："其养民也惠，其使民也义。" **力政**：以力服人的政治。力，力气，威力。《诗经·邶风·简兮》."有力如虎，执辔如组。"《商君书·刀塞》："汤武致强，而征诸侯，服其力也。"《孟子·公孙丑上》："以力服人者，非心服也，力不赡也；以德服人者，中心悦而诚服也，如七十子之服孔子也。"墨子讲"以义服人"，孟子讲"以德服人"，可以看出儒墨之不同观点。

【译文】

顺从天意的政治是以义服人的政治，违背天意的政治是以力服人的政治。

虽有贤君，不爱无功之臣

The virtuous ruler does not favour ministers without merit.

老人家说系列丛书

墨子说

虽有贤君，不爱无功之臣，虽有慈父，不爱无益之子。是故不胜其任而处其位，非此位之人也；不胜其爵而处其禄，非此禄之主也。

《墨子·亲士》

The virtuous ruler does not favour ministers without merit, the affectionate father dislikes sons of no use. He who occupies a position but is not equal to the job is not the right person for the position. He who draws the stipend but does not deserve his rank is not the right receiver of the stipend.

【注释】

无功之臣：墨子认为无功于国的臣子不应享受俸禄。《诗经·魏风·伐檀》："在位贪鄙，无功而受禄。"**不胜其爵而处其禄**：不能胜任那个爵位的工作而享受那个爵位的俸禄。爵，爵位。《礼记·王制》："王者之制禄爵，公、侯、伯、子、男凡五等。"注："禄，所受食，爵，秩次也。"

【译文】

贤君不欣赏无功之臣，慈父不喜欢无用之子。因此，不能胜任却占据那个职位，他就不该是这个位子上的人；不胜其爵位却领取其俸禄，他就不该是这种俸禄的主人。

所为贵良宝者，可以利民也

Treasures are to be valued for they can benefit the people.

所为贵良宝者，可以利民也，而义可以利人，故曰：义，天下之良宝也。

《墨子·耕柱》

Treasures are to be valued for they can benefit the people. Righteousness can benefit the people, so it is a treasure of the world to be highly valued.

【注释】

良宝：珍宝。良，精善。《吕氏春秋·仲冬纪》："陶器必良。"宝，珍贵之物。《墨子·七患》："食者，国之宝也。"《吕氏春秋·异宝》："子以玉为宝，我以不受为宝。"利民：使民得利。义，天下之良宝也：义是天下值得珍视的宝物。《墨子·天志上》："天下有义则生，无义则死；有义则富，无义则贫；有义则治，无义则乱。"

【译文】

宝物之所以值得珍视，是因为它可以让民众得到好处，而义是可以让民众得到好处的，所以说义是天下值得珍视的宝物。

太上无败，其次败而有以成

The best thing is to have no failure. The next best thing is to turn failure into success.

太上无败，其次败而有以成，此之谓用民。

《墨子·亲士》

The best thing is to have no failure. The next best thing is to turn failure into success, and this is deemed as the right employment of the people.

【注释】

墨子说：从前晋文公被迫出逃流亡于外十九年，后来却能重用贤才回国即位。齐桓公做国君前曾被迫出奔莒国，后来任用管仲称霸诸侯。越王勾践曾被吴王打败，于是卧薪尝胆，励精图治，终于在范蠡与文种等贤臣的帮助下消灭吴国，成为春秋霸主之一。所以说："太上无败，其次败而有以成。" **太上无败**：最好是不失败。太上，最上，最好。《韩非子·说疑》："是故禁奸之法，太上禁其心，其次禁其言，其次禁其事。"

【译文】

最好是不失败，其次是失败了却还有办法成功，这才叫善于用人。

天地不昭昭，大水不潦潦

Heaven and earth do not boast that they are bright and broad, great bodies of water do not boast that they are vast and boundless.

天地不昭昭，大水不潦潦，大火不燎燎，王德不尧尧者，乃千人之长也。

《墨子·亲士》

Heaven and earth do not boast that they are bright and broad, great bodies of water do not boast that they are vast and boundless, great fires do not boast that they are intense and blazing. The imperial rulers are not boastful of their virtues and merits, which makes them great rulers.

【注释】

昭昭（zhāozhāo）：明亮。屈原《九歌·云中君》："灵连蜷兮既留，烂昭昭兮未央。"《史记·天官书》："昭昭有光，利行兵。"**潦潦**（lǎolǎo）：雨水浩大。也指雨后的大水。《礼记·曲礼上》："水潦降，不献鱼鳖。"**燎燎**（liǎoliǎo）：明显的样子。《韩诗列传》二："诗之于事也，昭昭乎若日月之光明，燎燎乎如星辰之错行。"**尧尧**（yáoyáo）：崇高的样子。**千人之长**：天下的领袖。千，表示多。《韩非子·难二》："败军之诛，以千百数，犹北且不止。"长（zhǎng），位高者。《尚书·益稷》："外薄四海，咸建五长。"

【译文】

天地不自夸其明亮，大水不自夸其浩瀚，大火不自夸其炎烈，有德之君不自夸其德行高远，这样的人才能做天下的领袖。

天下从事者，不可以无法仪

To accomplish anything whatsoever one must have standards.

天下从事者，不可以无法仪。无法仪而其事能成者，无有也。

《墨子·法仪》

To accomplish anything whatsoever one must have standards. There are none that are able to accomplish anything without standards.

【注释】

墨子认为做任何事情都要有法度。百工画方形用矩，画圆形用规，画直线用墨绳，测偏正用悬垂。就是以矩、规、绳、悬垂作为法度。治国平天下更应该依靠法度。**从事**：办事、处理事务。《诗经·小雅·十月之交》："黾勉从事，不敢告劳。"**法仪**：法度。《管子·兵法》："治众有数，胜敌有理，……则可以定威德，制法仪，出号令，然后可以一众治民。"

【译文】

天下做任何事情都不能没有法度。没有法度就能把事情做成功的人，是没有的。

天下兼相爱则治，交相恶则乱

When there is universal love in the world, the world will be peaceful, and when there is mutual hatred in the world, the world will be chaotic.

天下兼相爱则治，交相恶则乱。故子墨子曰不可以不劝爱人者，此也。

《墨子·兼爱上》

When there is universal love in the world, the world will be peaceful, and when there is mutual hatred in the world, the world will be chaotic. This is why Mo Zi insisted on persuading people to love others.

【注释】

兼相爱：互相关爱。"兼相爱，交相利"，墨子主张爱无差等，不分厚薄亲疏，反对儒家的爱有差等说。交相恶：互相憎恶。爱人：爱护和帮助别人。《礼记·檀弓上》："君子之爱人也以德，细人之爱人也以姑息。"爱，亲爱。《左传·隐公三年》："兄爱弟敬。"墨子说："夫爱人者，人必从而爱之。"

【译文】

天下人互相关爱就太平，互相憎恶就混乱。所以墨子说为此不能不劝人相爱。

天下有义则生，无义则死

With righteousness, the world thrives; without it, the world will meet its demise.

天下有义则生，无义则死；有义则富，无义则贫；有义则治，无义则乱。

《墨子·天志上》

With righteousness, the world thrives; without it, the world will meet its demise. With it, the world is prosperous; without it, the world is impoverished. With it, the world is orderly; without it the world is chaotic.

【注释】

墨子接下来说："然则天欲其生而恶其死，欲其富而恶其贫，欲其治而恶其乱，此我所以知天欲义而恶不义也。"墨子认为天是有意志的，这也是墨子思想逻辑的起点。墨子贵义，说"万事莫贵于义"，甚至认为义比生命更贵重。义：宜，适宜。合理、适宜的事称义。《易·乾》："利物足以和义，贞固足以干事。"疏："言天能利益庶物，使物各得其宜。"孔子认为"义"和不正当的"利"相对立，"君子喻于义，小人喻于利"（《论语·里仁》），"不义而富且贵，于我如浮云"（《论语·述而》）。因此必须"见利思义"（《宪问》）、"见得思义"（《季氏》）。后儒对孔子思想作了发挥，思孟学派认为"义者宜也"（《中庸》），《荀子·荣辱》："义之所在，不倾于权，不顾其利。"南宋朱熹认为，"义者，天理之所宜"（《论语集注》）。

【译文】

天下有义人就生存，无义人就死亡；有义人就富贵，无义人就贫贱；有义社会就安定，无义社会就混乱。

天下之百姓皆上同于天子，而不上
同于天

If the multitudes only obey the Son of Heaven but not the will of Heaven ...

墨子说

天下之百姓皆上同于天子，而不
上同于天，则菑犹未去也。

《墨子·尚同上》

If the multitudes only obey the Son of Heaven but not
the will of Heaven, disasters will not be fully avoided.

【注释】

墨子主张"尚同"，尚同就是下级对上级的绝对服从。一里之人要服从于里长，一乡之人要服从于乡长，一国之人要服从于国君，天下之人要服从于天子。他认为"尚同"就不会产生祸乱，但又认为最高的意志是"天"，最后裁定是非的应该是天意而不是天子。菑（zāi）：灾害。同"灾"。《诗经·大雅·生民》："不坼不副，无菑无害。"

【译文】

天下老百姓如果只是服从天子而不是听命于天的意志，那么灾祸就不会完全避免。

天下之人皆相爱，强不执弱，众不
劫寡

When all the people in the world love one another，
the powerful will not control the vulnerable and the many
will not loot the few.

墨子说

天下之人皆相爱，强不执弱，众不劫寡，富不侮贫，贵不敖贱，诈不欺愚。

《墨子·兼爱中》

When all the people in the world love one another, the powerful will not control the vulnerable, the many will not loot the few, the wealthy will not bully the poor, the honoured will not disdain the humble, and the cunning will not deceive the simple-minded.

【注释】

天下之人皆相爱：这是墨子的最高理想，天下大治，必须兼爱，这是"天道"。执（zhí）：控制。《淮南子·主术》："故法律度量者，人主之所以执下，释而不用，是犹无辔衔而驰也。"劫（jié）：强取，抢夺。侮（wǔ）：欺负，凌辱。《诗经·大雅·烝民》："不侮矜寡，不畏强御。"敖（ào）：傲慢。通"傲"。《礼记·曲礼上》："敖不可畏，欲不可从。"《荀子·强国》："凡人好敖慢小事。"诈不欺愚：好行诈的人不欺骗弱智的人。诈（zhà），欺骗，假装。《左传·宣公十五年》："宋及楚平，华元为质。盟曰：'我无尔诈，尔无我虞。'"愚（yú），蠢笨，无知。《诗经·大雅·抑》："人亦有言，靡哲不愚。"

【译文】

天下人互相友爱，强者不会控制弱者，人多势众也不会劫掠势单力薄者，富有的人不会欺侮贫穷的人，显贵不会傲视低贱的人，好行诈的人不会欺骗弱智的人。

天下之所以乱者，其说将何哉

What is the reason for disorder in the world?

墨子说

天下之所以乱者，其说将何哉？则是天下士君子皆明于小而不明于大也。何以知其明于小不明于大也？以其不明于天之意也。

《墨子·天志下》

What is the reason for disorder in the world? It is because the gentlemen of the world all understand trifles, but not things of importance. How do we know they understand trifles but not things of importance? It's because they do not understand the will of Heaven.

【注释】

墨子曰："今天下之士君子，皆明于天子之正天下也，而不明于天之正天子也。"所以说：天下的士人君子明白小道理，而不明白大道理。墨子认为，天子虽然可以匡正天下，但也不能放任自己，因为上天是要匡正天子的。**士君子**，旧指有志操和学问的人。《荀子·修身》："士君子不为贫穷怠乎道。"**明于小而不明于大**：明白小道理而不明白大道理。小，小道理。这里指天子匡正天下的道理。大，大道理。这里指上天匡正天子的道理。**天之意**：上天的意志。墨子认为天是有意志的，一切以天之意志为法。

【译文】

当今天下混乱不堪，究竟是为什么呢？这是因为当今天下的士人君子，都明白小道理而不明白大道理。怎么知道他们只明白小道理而不明白大道理呢？是从他们不明白上天的意志知道的。

天下之所以生者，以先王之道教也

The world survives because the teachings of the ancient virtuous kings are heeded.

墨子说

天下之所以生者，以先王之道教也。今誉先王，是誉天下之所以生也。

《墨子·耕柱》

The world survives because the teachings of the ancient virtuous kings are heeded. To praise the sage kings is to praise the way that the world survives and thrives.

【注释】

儒家巫马子对墨子说："舍弃当今的人而去称颂先王，这是在称颂枯骨啊。就像木匠一样，只知道干枯的木头，却不懂得活生生的树木。"墨子对他说了上面的话后又说："该称颂而不称颂，就是不仁。"生：活着。与"死"相对。《诗经·邶风·击鼓》："生死契阔，与子成说。"《论语·先进》："未知生，焉知死？"先王：古代圣明天子。《论语·学而》："礼之用，和为贵。先王之道，斯为美。小大由之。"《孟子·梁惠王下》："吾何修而可以比于先王观也？"

【译文】

天下之所以能够生存，是因为接受了古代圣明天子的教化。现在人们称颂先王，就是称颂天下所赖以生存的天道。

天子为善，天能赏之

When a ruler practicses virtue, Heaven rewards him.

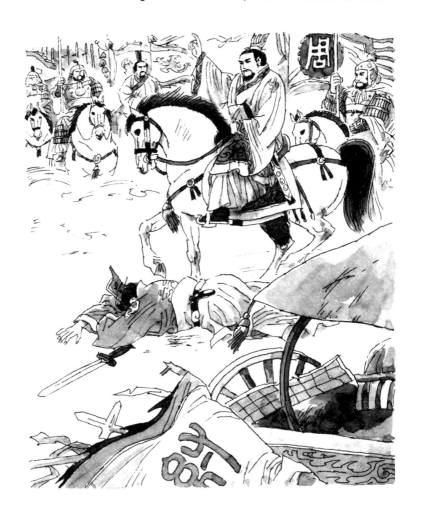

天子为善，天能赏之；天子为暴，天能罚之。

《墨子·天志中》

When a ruler practises virtue, Heaven rewards him; when a ruler tyrannizes, Heaven punishes him.

【注释】

墨子认为天子治理天下也不能放任自己的意志胡做非为，因为上天在时时匡正他的行为。从前夏、商、周三代圣王禹、汤、周文王、周武王，他们施政顺从天意，被称为"天德，聚敛天下之美名而加之焉，曰：此仁也，义也，爱人利人，顺天之意，得天之赏者也"。相反，三代暴君夏桀、商纣、周幽王、周厉王，他们施政违背天意，被称为"天贼，聚敛天下之丑名而加之焉，曰：此非仁也，非义也，憎人贼人，反天之意，得天之罚者也"。

【译文】

执政者施行善政，会受到上天的奖赏；施行暴政，会受到上天的惩罚。

天子者，天下之穷贵也，天下之穷
富也

The Son of Heaven is the most esteemed of the world
and the wealthiest of the world.

老人家说系列丛书

天子者，天下之穷贵也，天下之穷富也。故欲富且贵者，当天意而不可不顺。

《墨子·天志上》

The Son of Heaven is the most esteemed of the world and the wealthiest of the world. Therefore, if one wishes to be both esteemed and wealthy, he cannot but follow the will of Heaven.

【注释】

穷贵：最尊贵。穷，终极。《荀子·富国》："纵欲而不穷，则民心奋而不可说也。"当天意而不可不顺：墨子认为，顺从天意的人，互相关爱，交相得利，必定会得到赏赐；违背天意的人，互相厌恶，交相残害，必定会受到惩罚。他认为三代的圣王禹、汤、周文王、周武王是顺从天意的人；三代的暴君夏桀、商纣、周幽王、周厉王是违背了天意的人。

【译文】

天子是全天下最尊贵的人，也是天下最富有的人。所以想要大富大贵的人，不能不顺从天意。

天之行广而无私，其施厚而不德

Heaven is all inclusive and impartial, and abundant in its blessings without asking for gratitude.

墨子说

天之行广而无私，其施厚而不德，其明久而不衰，故圣王法之。

《墨子·法仪》

Heaven is all inclusive and impartial, and abundant in its blessings without asking for gratitude; Heaven is wise and its guidance ever lasting. This is why the sage kings accepted Heaven as their standard and followed its will.

【注释】

墨子提出"法天"的观点，因为在墨子看来，父母、老师、国君三者都是有缺点的，都谈不上兼爱，都不能成为效法的对象。只有天是无私的，因而是兼爱的。所以"莫若法大"。行：道的意思。施：恩惠。《易·乾》："见龙在田，德施普也。"不德：不感恩戴德。《孙膑兵法·行篡》："货多则辨，辨则民不德其上。"辨，通"便"。安逸。法：效法。《易·系辞上》："崇效天，卑法地。"

【译文】

天道博大无私，它施恩深厚却不让人民感恩戴德，它永久光明永不衰竭，所以圣明的君主都效法它。

为义而不能，必无排其道

When righteousness cannot be achieved, one must not complain about righteousness and abandon the way.

为义而不能，必无排其道。譬若匠人之斲而不能，无排其绳。

《墨子·贵义》

When righteousness cannot be achieved, one must not complain about righteousness and abandon the way, just as the carpenter must not blame the line of his ink when he cannot shape the timber straight.

【注释】

为义而不能，必无排其道：行义不能进行，不要埋怨道义。排，一说"排"当为"罪"字之误。罪，归罪于。《孟子·梁惠王上》："王无罪岁，斯天下之民至焉。"一说"排"为"诽"之借字。诽，毁谤。《庄子·刻意》："刻意尚行，离世异俗，高论怨诽，为亢而已矣。"注："非世无道，怨己不遇。"其实，"排"按本意"推移"解即可通，何必疑来疑去。斲（zhuó）：砍削。绳：木工画直线的工具。即墨线。《尚书·说命上》："惟木从绳则正，后从谏则圣。"

【译文】

墨子对他的几个弟子说："行义不能进行时，不要埋怨道义。就好像木匠砍削木头砍不正的时候决不会怪罪绳墨。"

我有天志，譬若轮人之有规，匠人之有矩

I understand the will of Heaven, like the wheelwright understands the compass, and the carpenter understands the square.

我有天志，譬若轮人之有规，匠人之有矩。

《墨子·天志上》

I understand the will of Heaven, like the wheelwright understands the compass, and the carpenter understands the square, so I am able to rule the world with wisdom.

【注释】

天志：上天的意志。古人认为天是有意志的神，是万物的主宰。《尚书·泰誓上》："天祐下民作之君，作之师。"天的意志是什么呢？墨子说："天之意，不欲大国之攻小国也，大家之乱小家也。强之劫弱，众之暴寡，诈之谋愚，贵之傲贱，此天之所不欲也。不止此而已，欲人之有力相营，有道相教，有财相分也。"轮人之有规：制造车轮的人掌握了画圆的工具。《墨子·天志中》："今夫轮人操其规，将以量度天下之圆与不圆也，曰：'中吾规者谓之圆，不中吾规者谓之不圆。'是以圆与不圆，皆可得而知也。"匠人之有矩：技工掌握了画方的工具。也指木工为匠人。《墨子·天志中》："匠人亦操其矩，将以量度天下之方与不方也，曰：'中吾矩者谓之方，不中吾矩者谓之不方。'是以方与不方，皆可得而知之。"

【译文】

我掌握了天的意志，就像做车轮的人掌握了画圆的工具，技工掌握了画方的工具一样，可以治理天下。

吾以为古之善者则述之，今之善者
则作之

I believe what was good in past times should be inherited and passed on. What is good in the present
should also be carried on.

墨子说

吾以为古之善者则述之，今之善者则作之，欲善之益多也。

《墨子·耕柱》

I believe what was good in past times should be inherited and passed on. What is good in the present should be also be carried on, and the purpose is a continuing increase of good.

【注释】

儒家之士公孟子对墨子说："君子不作，述而已。"意思是说君子阐述古意，并不创作。儒家是主张"述而不作"的。《论语·述而》："子曰：'述而不作，信而好古。'"孔子又曰："盖有不知而作之者，我无是也。"墨子则主张述、作不可偏废，皆务为其善而已。述而又作，则善益多矣。

【译文】

墨子说："我认为对古代好的东西要阐述继承，对现在好的东西则发扬光大，不过是希望好的东西越来越多罢了。"

多言而缓行，虽辩必不听

He who talks much but is slow in action will not be listened to, even though he is discerning.

务言而缓行，虽辩必不听；多力而伐功，虽劳必不图。

《墨子·修身》

He who talks much but is slow in action will not be listened to, even though he is discerning. He will not accomplish anything, who is capable but likes to boast of his feats, even though he labours hard.

【注释】

这是墨子提出的修身原则之一。他认为聪明人心明而不多说，有功劳而不自夸，反而能名扬天下。**务言而缓行**：说得多做得少。务言：致力于空谈。务，致力，从事。《管子·牧民》："不务地利，则仓廪不盈。"《论语·学而》："君子务本，本立而道生。"言，说话，言论。《论语·公冶长》："听其言而观其行。"**辩**：辩论，有口才。《孟子·滕文公下》："予岂好辩哉？予不得已也。"引申为巧言，诡辩。《老子》第81章："善者不辩，辩者不善。"**伐功**：夸耀自己的功劳。《论语·雍也》："孟之反不伐。"**图**：图谋，这里是认可的意思。

【译文】

说得多做得少的人，虽说得好听也无人肯信；出力虽多而好自夸功劳的人，虽然很辛苦也无人认可。

兴天下之利，除天下之害

Benefits for the people are promoted, harms for the world are eliminated.

兴天下之利，除天下之害，令国家百姓之不治也，自古及今，未尝之有也。

《墨子·节葬下》

It has never happened, from ancient times to the present day, that benefits for the people are promoted, harms for the world are eliminated, yet the country and the people are unable to be governed.

【注释】

兴天下之利：兴办对天下有益的大事。兴，兴起，发动。《礼记·乐记》："明于天地，然后能兴礼乐也。"利，利益，功用。《商君书·算地》："利出于地，则民尽力。"《战国策·秦策一》："大王之国，西有巴蜀汉中之利。"除天下之害：去除对天下有害的灾祸。除，去掉。《尚书·泰誓下》："除恶务本。"害，灾害，祸患。《墨子·尚同中》："将以为万民兴利除害。"《左传·隐公元年》："都城过百雉，国之害也。"

【译文】

兴办天下之大利，去除天下之大害，却不能让国家百姓得到治理，这样的事从古至今，从未有过。

言必立仪

To express one's view, one needs to establish and adhere to some standard.

言必立仪，言而毋仪，譬犹运钧之上而立朝夕者也，是非利害之辨，不可得而明知也。

《墨子·非命上》

To express one's view, one needs to establish and adhere to some standard. If there is no standard, it is similar to putting the sundial on a revolving potter's wheel to determine the time of day, and the time cannot be known.

【注释】

言必立仪：发表言论一定要先树立一个标准。立，树立。如言：立德、立功、立言等。仪，法度，标准。《国语·周语下》："度之于轨仪。"《淮南子·修务》："设仪立度，可以为法则。"毋：无，没有。运钧：古代制作陶器时用的转轮。运，转也。高诱注《淮南子》云："钧，陶人作瓦器法，下转旋者。"朝夕：即日晷，古代用日影以测量时间的仪器。《管子·七法》："不明于则，而欲出号令，犹立朝夕于运均之上。"唐房玄龄注："均，陶者之轮。立朝夕所以正东西也。"在有刻度的盘中央立一根与盘垂直的棍的装置叫日晷，利用太阳投射的影子测定时间。如果把它立在转轮之上是无法测定时间的。

【译文】

发表言论，一定要先树立一个标准，如果没有标准，就好像把日晷放到制作陶器的转轮上一样，是无法测定时间的。

言必有三表

To express one's view, one needs to follow three principles.

言必有三表。何谓三表？子墨子言曰：有本之者，有原之者，有用之者。

《墨子·非命上》

To express one's view, one needs to follow three principles. What are the three principles? Mo Zi said：to probe into the nature of things，to study the reason of things，and to apply these to one's practices.

【注释】

墨子提出的"三表法"，即判断是非标准，要遵循"本、原、用"三原则。"于何本之？上本之于古者圣王之事。于何原之？下原察百姓耳目之实。于何用之？废以为刑政，观其中国家百姓人民之利。此所谓言有三表也。"三表：三项法则。表，标准，法则。《淮南子·本经》："戴圆履方，抱表怀绳。"**有本之者**：用天帝鬼神的意志和圣王的行事来考察其本质。**有原之者**：用先王的书籍记载来验证其义理。**有用之者**：把它用到刑罚政令的实践中去。

【译文】

发表言论有三条必须遵循的法则。哪三条法则呢？墨子说：审查本质，推究情理，用于实践。

言足以复行者，常之

Doctrines proven feasible through practice over and again can be advocated.

言足以复行者，常之；不足以举行者，勿常。不足以举行而常之，是荡口也。

《墨子·耕柱》

Doctrines proven feasible through practice over and again can be advocated; doctrines proven unfeasible shall not be advocated. If doctrines unfeasible are advocated, they are merely empty words.

【注释】

复行：通过多次行动验证。复，再，又一次。《左传·僖公五年》："晋侯复假道虞以伐虢。"行（xíng），行为。《论语·公冶长》："今吾于人也，听其言而观其行。"常：通"尚"，崇尚。举：行动。《左传·庄公二十三年》："君举必书，书而不发，后嗣何观？"荡口：空话，不可行而空言。荡，放纵。《尚书·毕命》："以荡陵德，实悖天道。"《论语·阳货》："古之狂也肆，今之狂也荡。"

【译文】

言论经实践验证可行的话，就崇尚它；如果言论不能实行，就不要崇尚它。不能实行却又受到崇尚的言论，就是空话。

言无务为多而务为智，无务为文而
务为察

**In speech, it is not quantity but ingenuity, not elo-
quence but insight, that counts.**

言无务为多而务为智，无务为文而务为察。

《墨子·修身》

In speech, it is not quantity but ingenuity, not eloquence but insight, that counts.

【注释】

言：说话。《论语·先进》："夫人不言，言必有中。"智：机智，谋略。《史记·项羽本纪》："吾宁斗智，不能斗力。"文：美，善。《礼记·乐记》："礼减而进，以进为文；乐盈而反，以反为文。"察：昭著，明显。《礼记·中庸》："《诗》云：'鸢飞戾天，鱼跃于渊'，言其上下察也。"

【译文】

话不在多而在于机智，不在文雅而在明察。

衣食者，人之生利也

Clothing and food are the necessities of life.

衣食者，人之生利也，然且犹尚有节；葬埋者，人之死利也，夫何独无节于此乎？

《墨子·节葬下》

Even clothing and food, which are the necessities of life, should be consumed in frugality. How then can funerals and burials, which are the necessities of death, be conducted in extravagance?

【注释】

墨子说：当时社会上王公大人死后埋葬，必有棺有椁，还有纹饰的皮革缠结多遍，大量的玉器、铜器、陶器随葬，装裹衣服被褥无数，并有车马女乐殉葬，地下墓室建造豪华，地上封树雄伟高大如山陵。生利：人活着时的利益。生，活。和"死"相对。《论语·先进》："未知牛，焉知死。"利，利益。《商君书·算地》："利出于地，则民尽力。"有节：有所节制。节，节制，节约。《易·颐》："君子以慎言语，节饮食。"《墨子·节葬下》："如彼则大厚，如此则大薄，然则葬埋之有节矣。"死利：人死后的利益。

【译文】

衣食是人们活着的时候所必需的利益，尚且要节约；葬埋是人们死后所需要的利益，为什么却单单不要节制呢？

179

以德就列，以官服事

Ranks should be arranged according to virtue, tasks assigned according to office.

以德就列，以官服事，以劳殿赏，量功而分禄。

《墨子·尚贤上》

Ranks should be arranged according to virtue, tasks assigned according to office, rewards granted according to performance, and pay given according to merits.

【注释】

墨子认为把爵位、俸禄和决断权交给贤人，不是对贤人的赏赐，而是为他们提供做事成功的条件。**以德就列**：以德行安排爵位高低。列，列次，次第。《淮南子·诠言》："俎豆之列次，黍稷之先后，虽知弗教也。"**殿**：定。有的版本"殿"作"受"。按成绩受赏赐，意更明。**量**：衡量。《左传·隐公十一年》："度德而处之，量力而行之。"

【译文】

以德行安排爵位，按职权管理政事，按成绩接受封赏，依功劳定俸禄。

义者，善政也

Governance with righteousness is good governance.

义者，善政也。何以知义之善政
也？曰：天下有义则治，无义则乱，
是以知义之善政也。

《墨子·天志中》

Governance with righteousness is good governance. How
do we know that governance with righteousness is good? Because with righteousness the world will be orderly, and without it the world will be chaotic. Therefore governance with
righteousness is good.

【注释】

墨子认为"天欲义而恶不义"。怎么知道上天喜欢义而厌恶不义呢？回答是：天
下有义的人生存，无义的人死亡；有义者富贵，无义者贫贱；有义者安定，无义者
混乱。而上天希望人类生存而不希望人类死亡，希望人类富有而不希望人类贫贱，
希望社会安定而不希望社会混乱，这就是我所知道的上天喜欢义而厌恶不义的原因。
善政：妥善的法则政令。《左传·宣公十二年》："见可而进，知难而退，军之善
政也。"

【译文】

以义服人的政治就是好的政治。怎么知道以义服人
的政治就是好的政治呢？天下有义就安定，无义就混
乱，以此知道以义服人的政治就是好的政治。

义者政也

Righteousness means right and justifiable.

老人家说系列丛书

墨子说

义者政也，无从下之政上，必从
上之政下。

《墨子·天志上》

Righteousness means right and justifiable. It is not to be
given by the subordinates to the superior, but by the superior
to the subordinates.

【注释】

义者政也：义就是匡正的意思。政，恰好。《墨子·节葬下》："上稽之尧舜禹汤
文武之道，而政逆之；下稽之桀纣幽厉之事，犹合节也。"政，纠正，通"正"。
《论语·尧曰》："君子正其衣冠。"《论语·学而》："君子食无求饱，居无求安，敏
于事而慎于言，就有道而正焉，可谓好学也已。"无从下之政上：墨子认为：不能以
下正上，必须以上正下。士人匡正普通人，将军、大夫匡正士人，三公、诸侯匡正
将军、大夫，天子匡正三公、诸侯，上天匡正天子。天下事都是由天意主持的。

【译文】

义就是匡正的意思，不能以下正上，必须以上
正下。

185

原浊者流不清，行不信者名必耗

As a muddy source generates a stream not clear,
unfaithful conduct tarnishes one's fame.

原浊者流不清，行不信者名必耗。名不徒生而誉不自长，功成名遂。

《墨子·修身》

As a muddy source generates a stream not clear, un-faithful conduct tarnishes one's fame. Reputation does not spring up out of nothing, nor does praise grow by itself. Reputation follows upon success.

【注释】

原：水源。同"源"。《左传·昭公九年》："犹衣服之有冠冕，木水之有本原。" 耗（hào）：同"耗"。败坏的意思。**名不徒生而誉不自长**：名声不会凭空而来，赞誉也不会自己提高。徒，副词。空，徒然。《玉台新咏·古诗为焦仲卿妻作》："妾不堪驱使，徒留无所施。" **功成名遂**：建立了功业，成就了名声。《淮南子·道应训》："功成名遂身退，天之道也。"

【译文】

源头混浊水流不会清澈，行为不守信用的人名誉必然会败坏。名声不会凭空而来，赞誉也不会自己提高。只有成就了功业，名声才会到来。

谮慝之言，无入之耳

Do not listen to any treacherous words.

老人家说系列丛书

墨子说

谮慝之言，无入之耳；批扞之声，无出之口；杀伤人之孩，无存之心。虽有诋讦之民，无所依矣。

《墨子·修身》

Do not listen to any treacherous words, do not utter any defamatory words, do not entertain any idea of hurting others. Then, even if there are evil-minded persons who spread discord, they will lose their support.

【注释】

谮慝之言：诬蔑毁谤的坏话。谮（zèn），诬陷。《诗经·小雅·巷伯》："彼谮人者，亦已大甚。"慝（tè），邪恶。《尚书·大禹谟》："（舜）负罪引慝，祇载见瞽瞍。"注："慝，恶也。"批扞之声：恶毒攻击别人的话。扞（hàn），触犯。亦作"捍"。杀伤人之孩：伤害别人的想法。孩，一说应为"刻"。诋讦之民：搬弄是非的人。诋（dǐ），诬蔑，毁谤。《汉书·刘向传》："是以群小窥见间隙，巧言丑诋，流言飞文，哗于民间。"讦（jié），发人隐私。《论语·阳货》："恶不逊以为勇者，恶讦以为直者。"依：依靠。《国语·晋语二》："托在草莽，未有所依。"

【译文】

对于诬陷人的话，不要听；诽谤人的话，不要说；害人之心不可有。这样，虽然有专门搬弄是非的人，也就无处依托了。

争一言以相杀，是贵义于其身也

One would rather die than give away righteousness.
This shows righteousness is even more valuable than
one's life.

老人家说系列丛书

争一言以相杀，是贵义于其身也。故曰：万事莫贵于义也。

《墨子·贵义》

One would rather die than give away righteousness. This shows righteousness is even more valuable than one's life. Hence we say that of the multitude of things one possesses, none is more valuable than righteousness.

【注释】

争一言以相杀：为争义而选择死亡。一言，即指义。相，选择。杀，死。《汉书·伍被传》："男子之所死者，一言耳。"一言，指义。《吕氏春秋·上德》："墨者钜子孟胜曰：死之所以行墨者之义而继其业者也。"**贵义**：看重义。贵，重视。《礼记·中庸》："去谗远色，贱货而贵德。"

【译文】

为争义而选择死亡，这是因为义比生命更可贵。所以说，世间没有比义更可宝贵的事了。

191

政者，口言之，身必行之

To govern is to apply what one advocates to one's actions.

政者，口言之，身必行之。

《墨子·公孟》

To govern is to apply what one advocates to one's actions.

【注释】

告子对墨子说："我能够治理国政。"墨子说："治理国政，不仅是嘴里说说，还得亲身做到。现在你只是空口白话，自己并不去做，你连自己都管不好，怎么能管理好国家呢？"言：说话。《论语·先进》："夫人不言，言必有中。"行：实行。《论语·先进》："冉有问：'闻斯行诸？'子曰：'闻斯行之。'"

【译文】

所谓治政，不仅是口头说，还必须亲自做到。

执无鬼而学祭礼，是犹无客而学客
礼也

To hold that there are no spirits, yet still learn sacrificial ceremonies is similar to learning the etiquette of
hospitality while having no guests.

老人家说系列丛书　墨子说

执无鬼而学祭礼，是犹无客而学客礼也，是犹无鱼而为鱼罟也。

《墨子·公孟》

To hold there are no spirits, yet still learn sacrificial ceremonies is similar to learning the etiquette of hospitality while having no guests, or to making fishing nets while having no fish.

【注释】

墨子坚持让人相信鬼神的存在，他说："古者圣王皆以鬼神为神明，而为祸福，执有祥不祥，是以政治而国安也。"公孟子对他说："不存在鬼神。"但又说，"君子必须学习祭礼的礼仪。"墨子以此为据反对儒家的祭礼。执：坚持。《汉书·外戚传》："书奏，上以问光，光执不许。"罟（gǔ）：网。《易·系辞下》："（包牺氏）作结绳而为网罟，以佃以渔。"释文："取兽曰网，取鱼曰罟。"

【译文】

坚持鬼神不存在又去学习祭祀的礼仪，这好比明明知道没有客人却要学待客之礼，明明知道没有鱼却要织渔网一样。

195

志不强者智不达，言不信者行不果

One's wisdom will not be far-reaching if his will is not strong. One's action will not be resolute if he fails to keep his promises.

志不强者智不达，言不信者行不果。

《墨子·修身》

One's wisdom will not be far-reaching if his will is not strong. One's action will not be resolute if he fails to keep his promises.

【注释】

志：意志。《论语·子罕》："子曰：'三军可夺帅也，匹夫不可夺志也。'"此不可夺之志即指意志。智：才智。《国语·周语下》："言智必及事。"注："能处事物为智。"言不信者行不果：说话不守信用，行为不果敢。"言信行果"，是墨家主张为人处世的基本信条。《墨子·兼爱下》："言必信，行必果，使言行之合犹符节也，无言而不行也。"意谓言出必守信，行为必果断。也有言行必相符合的意思。《论语·子路》："言必信，行必果，砼砼然小人哉！"孔子虽也重信，但却把"言信行果"说成是"不问是非黑白的小人"坚守的准则。孟子则明谓："大人者言不必信，行不必果，惟义所在。"（《孟子·离娄下》）反映了儒墨两家在这一问题上的不同观点。

【译文】

意志不坚定的人才智不会通达，说话不守信用的人行为也不会果断。

治于神者，众人不知其功

The merit of the man who employs brilliant intelligence is not recognized by the multitudes.

治于神者，众人不知其功；争于明者，众人知之。

《墨子·公输》

The merit of the man who employs brilliant intelligence is not recognized by the multitudes. On the other hand, he who strives in the open is recognized.

【注释】

公输子（鲁班）为楚王造成攻城的云梯，准备攻打宋国。墨子疾行十日夜到达楚国，先见公输子陈说楚攻宋的结果是两败俱伤，又和他演练攻防之阵，公输子九次演练攻城之机变，均被墨子化解。公输子说："我知道用什么办法对付你了，但我不说。"墨子说："我知道你的办法就是杀掉我，宋国就无人守城了。可是在我来之前已布置弟子三百人在宋国城头上等着楚兵了。"最后楚王不得不放弃攻宋计划。墨于化解了宋亡国的危险，回来时路过宋国，天下起大雨，墨子想到里巷避雨，守门人却不让他进去。**神**：谓事理玄妙，神奇。《易·系辞上》："阴阳不测之谓神。"注："神也者，变化之极妙万物而为言，不可形诘者也。"**明**：显著，公开。《战国策·齐策一》："则秦不能害齐，亦已明矣。"

【译文】

运用神机妙算的人，众人不知道他的功劳；而参与明争的人，众人却都认得他。

自古以及今，生民以来者，亦尝有见命之物

From antiquity to the present, since the beginning of mankind, has anyone seen such a thing as fate?

自古以及今，生民以来者，亦尝有见命之物，闻命之声者乎？则未尝有也。

《墨子·非命中》

From antiquity to the present, since the beginning of mankind, has anyone heard the sound of fate or seen such a thing as fate? No, no one has.

【注释】

墨子的"非命论"是为了反对儒家的"生死有命，富贵在天"的天命论而提出的。他认为儒家的"天命论"是"繁饰有命以教众愚朴之人"，可谓一语中的，但又不可避免地和他的其他主张相矛盾。**生民**：人民。《孟子·公孙丑上》："率其子弟，攻其父母，自有生民以来，未有能济者也。"**物**：泛指天地间万物。《诗经·大雅·烝民》："天生烝民，有物有则。"此指物之形象。

【译文】

从古到今，自有人民以来，有人见过命的形象，听到过命的声音吗？从来没有过。

责任编辑：韩　颖
英　译：郭　辉
封面设计：胡　湖
印刷监制：佟汉冬

图书在版编目（CIP）数据

墨子说：汉英对照／蔡希勤编注．—北京：华语
教学出版社，2011
（老人家说系列）
ISBN 978－7－5138－0145－4

Ⅰ．①墨…　Ⅱ．①蔡…　Ⅲ．①汉语－对外汉语教学－
自学参考资料②墨家－汉、英　Ⅳ．①H195.4②B224

中国版本图书馆 CIP 数据核字（2011）第 161610 号

老人家说·墨子说

蔡希勤　编注

＊

ⓒ华语教学出版社
华语教学出版社出版
（中国北京百万庄大街 24 号　邮政编码 100037）
电话：（86）10－68320585　68997826
传真：（86）10－68997826　68326333
网址：www.sinolingua.com.cn
电子信箱：hyjx@sinolingua.com.cn
北京市松源印刷有限公司印刷
2011 年（大 32 开）第 1 版
（汉英）
ISBN 978－7－5138－0145－4
定价：35.00 元